GLOBAL MAGNA CARTA

Returning Power to the 99% ... if they want it!

J T Coombes

Global Magna Carta – Returning Power to the 99% ... if they want it!

J T Coombes

First published in Great Britain by J T Coombes Ltd, 2013

Global Magna Carta – www.globalmagnacarta.com

Typesetting by Quotes – www.quotes.uk.com

Cover by Sarah Medway – www.smedway.co.uk

Proofreading by Bridget Gevaux – www.abcproofreading.co.uk

Copyright Clearance by Rachel Thorne – www.rnpermissions.co.uk

A CIP record for this book is available from the British Library.

ISBN	Hardback	978-0-9927782-0-0
	Paperback	978-0-9927782-1-7
	eBook	978-0-9927782-2-4

We are born into essential goodness, endowed with natural intuitions about what is good and worthy and what is not.

EPICTETUS, GREEK PHILOSOPHER, AD 55–135

This book is dedicated to this beautiful Planet and its wonderful Inhabitants. Collectively, they taught me about myself, and the power of unconditional love.

JTC, OCTOBER 2013

Copyright Information and Disclaimer

I strive for accuracy but cannot be held responsible for any errors in quotations or incorrect attributions. Some quotations may include content considered inappropriate by some standards for some age groups. I take no responsibility for filtering content based on any standards of morality, religion, or politics.

The content of this book has evolved from copious reading and Internet research over the years and some of the many sources that have contributed to my forming the perspectives expressed here are listed at the beginning of this book. However, I leave it to each reader to 'Google' points of curiosity for verification, as I have done.

Acknowledgements

I am grateful to all of the organisations listed below for their kind permission to reproduce the following copyright material, none of which would have been possible without the dedicated professionalism of my copyright clearance advisor Rachel Thorne:

The Guardian for an extract from "Food shortages could force world into vegetarianism, warn scientists" by John Vidal, *The Guardian*, 26 August 2012, copyright © Guardian News and Media Ltd 2012; The Independent for an extract from "British politics at the crossroads: Tory membership plummets over disenchantment with Westminster" by Nigel Morris & Oliver Wright, in *The Independent* 9th August 2013, © The Independent, 2013, www.independent.co.uk; UNICEF for an extract from the UNICEF Mid-Year Review of 2010 Humanitarian Action Report, "Demographic and Health Survey (EMMUS) VI, 2005–2006". www.measuredhs.com/pubs/pdf/FR192/FR192.pdf. Reproduced with permission; Optomen Television Ltd for a list of "The New Ten Commandments", Channel Four News, 2005. Courtesy of Optomen Television; Kiva for company information, www.kiva.org. Reproduced with kind permission; Audur and Halla Tómasdóttir for information about Audur Capital and Sisters Capital respectively. Reproduced with kind permission; Deniz Kandiyoti for an extract from "Women make up half Not the Church, Not the State? Gender equality in the crossfire" by Deniz Kandiyoti 23 July 2010, http://www.opendemocracy.net. Reproduced with permission; and Merco Press for a quote from "Women make up half of the new Bolivian ministerial cabinet" 25 January 2010. http://en.mercopress.com. Reproduced with permission; and Richard Bater for an extract adapted from "Hope from below: composing the commons in Iceland" by Richard Bater, 1 December 2011, http://www.opendemocracy.net. Reproduced with permission.

This is also the appropriate place to pay tribute to James and Sarah, whose mention earlier simply as 'Typesetting' and 'Cover' does not do justice to their true contribution in helping me bring this work into the public domain.

I have known Sarah for many years and her creative gift never ceases to amaze and inspire me in all I do. James' previous experience in the publishing world has been the voice of guidance and reassurance that is constantly in the background as I take my first tentative steps into the many diverse activities that are the work of a publisher. I am deeply indebted to both of them.

Sources of Inspiration for this Book

The following are people and sources of information whose perceptions about Life have been an inspiration to my thinking over the years. I do not profess to be an expert on their work; indeed, on many occasions a book of 300 pages has yielded just one sentence that has greatly impacted my thinking and added another piece to the jigsaw of my philosophy. With the ageing process encouraging a more erratic memory, I am sure there will be omissions from this list, for which I most sincerely apologise.

People who influenced my thinking

Archimedes • Aristotle • David Attenborough • Marcus Aurelius • Sir Tim Berners-Lee • William Blake • Ellen Hodgson Brown • 'Capability' Brown • Winston Churchill • Cicero • Charles Darwin • Richard Dawkins • Charles Dickens • Albert Einstein • Epictetus • Sigmund Freud • Milton Friedman • Ghandi • Edward Gibbon • Friedrich Hayek • Joan of Arc • Helena Kennedy • John F Kennedy • John Maynard Keynes • Aung San Suu Kyi • Abraham Lincoln • James Lovelock • Nelson Mandela • Friedrich Nietzsche • Isaac Newton • Florence Nightingale • George Orwell • Jeremy Paxman • Pythagoras • George Soros • Theodore Roosevelt • Seneca • Adam Smith • Lao Tzu • Voltaire • Neale Donald Walsch • Elizabeth Warren • HRH The Prince of Wales

Organisations that have influenced my thinking

Alternet.org • Avaaz.org • 38degrees.org.uk • BBC News • Bill Bonner's Daily Reckoning at moneyweek.com • Bill Moyers • Newsletter.com • Chatham House • Club de Madrid • Conservation International • Friends of the Earth • Freepress.net • The Huffington Post • Global Economic Intersection • Google • Greenpeace • Investors Chronicle • Inter Press Service • In These Times • La Via Campesina • LiveScience • Naked Capitalism • OpEdNews.com • OneClimate – www.oneworld.org • openDemocracy.net • Open Europe • Open Society Foundations • Oxford Research Group • Pacific Whale Foundation • Slate.com • Smart Planet • TED.com • The Economist • Transition Network • The Center for Public Integrity • The Globalist • The Guardian.co.uk • The Independent & The Independent on Sunday • The New York Times • The Public Banking Institute • The Real News • The Scientist Magazine • The Sierra Club • The Thom Hartmann Program • The Wall Street Journal • TomDispatch.com • Truthout • Transparency International • Wikipedia • World Development Movement

People who have entered my Life, either for a few moments or years and, whether they realised it or not, made a huge contribution in helping me to get to know myself better ... and to whom I will be eternally grateful.

Andy • Ann • Bill • Bob • Charlie • Chris • Dan • Doris • Eric • Jen • JohnC • JohnG • JohnR • Kate • Lee • Margaret • Marylouise • Mike • Nicole • Peter • Richard • Rob • Sue • Tim • Tony • Trev • Wendy & David • Wendy • Winnie

Magna Carta and this Book in a Nutshell

The Problem – King John (1166–1216) was proclaimed King of England in 1199 and along with this title came lands in France. It was said that John had dangerous personality traits that exuded spitefulness and cruelty, evidenced in his mistreatment of French nobles that eventually resulted in the loss of these lands.

His subsequent failed attempts to regain them through continuous warfare resulted in his growing abuse of his subjects from the high taxation and futile loss of human life his obsession caused. Many of his nobles became increasingly discontent with this tyranny as he began imposing new taxes without their prior agreement, breaking with feudal law and customs of the times and bringing the country to its knees.

At the same time he also succeeded in angering the Roman Catholic Church and was excommunicated by the Pope in 1209.

The Solution – 1214 saw the nadir of John's reign. After yet another failed attempt to regain his French lands he returned to England to extract further taxes and a new army but was met by rebellion. After bloody altercations with his people, the nobles sat down with the king and negotiated 63 clauses that made up the first document which, *through the power of the written word*, would force the then elite to cease the abuse of the majority.

Magna Carta came into force on 15th June 1215. Of particular significance was a section now called clause 61, which established a committee of 25 nobles who oversaw what the king was up to. They had powers to overrule his will and even confiscate his property if he defied the dictates of the Charter.

The Outcome – Unfortunately Magna Carta was not an overnight success in curbing John's abuses, as he chose to ignore much of its contents up until his death a year later. However, his successor Henry III agreed the Charter's place in Society in 1225 and this was granted in perpetuity in 1237. For the next 600 years this famous Charter determined the manner in which those we give our power to governed Society, by defining and maintaining the rights and freedoms of the people.

This Charter remained intact until 1829 when clause 26 was repealed. With this action a precedent was created, and over the next 140 years the majority of the Charter was repealed, leaving just 3 clauses remaining after 1969.

> *With this loss we seem to be returning to the abuses of 800 years ago, begging the question as to whether a new updated version of this Charter is now needed … and "the nobles" to go with it. JTC*

FOREWORD

I once saw a cartoon that showed a Mayan priest etching out the famous Mayan Calendar on a round stone the size of a car wheel, with another priest looking on.

The first priest looks up and, in a resigned voice, says, 'That's it, I can't go any further. There's no more room.'

The second priest asks, 'What year have you got to?'

The first replies, '2012.'

The second priest retorts, 'That should have them crapping themselves!'

They both laugh.

I am sure that this story has as much credibility as the message given by the many doomsayers across the centuries, citing the Mayan Calendar as evidence of the ending of Civilisation.

Magna Carta (Great Charter), on the other hand, was no creation of fiction. Lord Denning (1899-1999), Master of the Rolls in the UK for over 20 years, and regarded by many lawyers as the greatest judge of the century, once described this Charter as 'the greatest constitutional document of all times – the foundation of the freedom of the individual against the arbitrary authority of the despot' (source: Wikipedia).

In the infancy of this second millennium, we are seeing the sentiment, size and determination of an increasing myriad of *peaceful* Resistance Movements growing across the Planet as people begin to take back their power. I believe that future generations will look back at this time and recognise that the myth of 2012 and the sentiment of Magna Carta were somehow inextricably entwined.

The challenges we now face as a species are wholly unprecedented in our history, both in number and their enormity of scale, as we try to accommodate and adapt to Globalisation, Multiculturalism and the rapid explosion of global Technology and Communications supporting the birthing of the Technological Age.

Traditional boundaries that have separated our species, by race, colour, creed and gender are being swept aside, along with the beliefs that have kept them in place for millennia. These very beliefs are now seen to be in a state of paralysis because of a lack of trust from within and outside of the institutions that promote them. Traditional thinking that is taking us to the edge of a financial and social abyss now appears unable to find solutions.

It was Albert Einstein who observed, and this is my interpretation of his wisdom, which I repeat throughout the book, and for which I make no apology:

The thinking that created the problem is incapable of solving it.

If Einstein's observation is correct, then the time has come for new thinking and leadership to extricate us from our own undoing, and positively move us forward.

This book argues that, only by understanding who and what we are, and how we function as a species, recognising our fallibilities as well as our fabulous talents, can we hope to arrest our current headlong journey to hell in a handcart!

It was this very omission, when drawing up the original Magna Carta all those centuries ago, that has now placed our species back at square one.

Back then, we only addressed the problem (the financial abuse of the 99% by the 1%) and not the cause (human fallibility). By recognising what we are all about, I believe we can break this circle of destruction that has always dogged our species.

> *I offer Global Magna Carta as a catalyst for creative thought in how we might change our world ... and watch the direction we take ... or not!* JTC

Armed with a greater understanding of how we function, we are capable of constructing a new Moral Code that returns to the people the power they have gradually handed back to our institutions since 1829. Its primary purpose would be to help us better interact with each other and this beautiful Planet, taking us into a whole new world ... the world of Global Magna Carta.

Author's Note

I am by no means qualified, nor desire to sit in judgement upon my fellow woman and man. None of my observations are offered as an indictment, but simply as a perspective, to stimulate debate that might lead to the changes we are now looking for and so desperately need.

It is a personal perception of Life that has come from devoting the last 25 years of my life to answering questions about the human condition (MY human condition); finally arriving at a conclusion that, only by changing traditional thinking, can we find solutions to the problems that earlier thinking created.

In writing this book, it has only ever been my intention to champion the cause that we are an incredible species, capable of creating whatever we set our minds to ... indeed, this is what we excel at ... **and now is the time to apply that genius to start rebuilding our broken Society and regain the full enjoyment we are entitled to in this thing called 'Life'.**

PERSONAL STATEMENT BY THE AUTHOR

In a time of Universal deceit, telling the truth is a revolutionary act.

(Although controversy continues today as to whether George Orwell actually said this or not, I believe its sentiment to be apposite to this Statement.)

As a child (born in South London in 1946) through to adolescence, I was mentally abused and manipulated by a caring mother struggling to deal with her own issues. This abuse culminated in my futile attack upon a woman of similar age to her a few months before my wedding. I was placed on Probation and the internal forces that fuelled that abusive assault disappeared during the incident and have never returned.

The wedding went ahead and, for more than 20 years, I worked hard in the City of London, with others, building companies, of which my most satisfying was a financial services group within 11 years of starting up, managing funds of nearly £100 million.

My personal drive came from a desire to give my family a good home and a good education for my children. In midlife (1987), however, I suffered a crisis, experiencing five of the top ten major life traumas – Burnout (M.E.), Breakdown, Loss of Home, Divorce, Bankruptcy.

Whilst, like anyone else, there are episodes in my life that I am not proud of, I am not a violent or physical person and try to live my life with integrity. I therefore found myself looking back upon a life influenced by Christian values with utter confusion, following the loss of that which I valued so much.

In consequence, I embarked upon a journey to find answers that would make sense of the personal chaos I had experienced. This led me to consider life as a whole, and who and what we are as a species.

A quarter of a century later, I have come to realise that fallibility is an inherent part of the human condition, capable of inflicting chaos upon both our loved ones and complete strangers with equal devastation. As an intrinsic part of us, our fallibilities need to be understood and accepted, allowing us then to manage them and thus eradicate or reduce their ability to *manage us*, and the ensuing misery this causes.

I am a 'Freethinker' and member of the human race. It is within this context that I make these personal observations on Life, in these troubling times of collapsing traditional institutions, suffocating global debt and imprisonment by terrorism. I am also driven to offer this work as a positive contribution to our development as a species – a right available to every single person on this Planet.

J T COOMBES, DECEMBER 2013

CONTENTS

OF PARTICULAR IMPORTANCE ...

The sentiments expressed in this book are not new ...

> *"The problems of the world cannot be solved by sceptics or cynics whose horizons are limited by the obvious realities. We need men (and women*) who can dream of things that never were."*
>
> PRESIDENT JOHN F KENNEDY, 1917–1963

> *"Since everything is a reflection of our minds, everything can be changed by our minds."*
>
> BUDDHA

> *'Never doubt that a small group of thoughtful committed citizens can change the world. Indeed, it is the only thing that ever has.'*
>
> (PARAPHRASED) MARGARET MEADE, 1901–1978

> *'First they ignore you. Then they laugh at you. Then they fight you. Then you win.'*
>
> MY INTERPRETATION OF A WISDOM ATTRIBUTED TO GANDHI, 1869–1948

> *'I called the New World into existence to redress the balance of the Old.'*
>
> GEORGE CANNING, BRITISH PRIME MINISTER, 1770–1827

The comments shown in italics within indented paragraphs that occur throughout the book are designed to help me emphasise points, and highlight thinking by learned people dating as far back as Ancient Greece. The subjects covered in this book have always been a part of 'the human experience'. The thinking here tries to bring awareness to how we function, by reiterating the unchanging wisdom of the Ancients which, the author believes, can contribute to rebuilding our Society by reassuring us when we lose our way in our group and individual journeys through Life.

**Author's insertion*

INTRODUCTION: A PERSONAL PERSPECTIVE ON LIFE IN THIS NEW MILLENNIUM

At the beginning of this 21st century, there is growing concern from the International community at the persistent efforts by countries such as Iran and North Korea to adopt a nuclear capability.

Whilst a part of me is totally in support of this concern, another part of me can see that every country that does not currently have it should be seeking this devastating capability … unless we can change our current beliefs and thinking!

We have created a world increasingly dominated by narrow financial beliefs and disciplines that prioritise financial reward as the purpose to any and all of our activities in Life, be they humanitarian, social, political or corporate. Since the Financial Crisis of 2007/08, these dominating disciplines have become increasingly less supportive of the basic needs of mankind. This is primarily because of growing global debt and the austerity measures imposed upon the 99% to reduce that debt.

It will be decades before we return to the financial solvency demanded by these disciplines and I increasingly question if we ever will, as our children begin to shoulder the responsibility for something they had no hand in creating.

Quite how they will achieve this in an environment where their education and employment potential is being seriously eroded, because of political priorities given to debt repayment, has not yet been answered.

This man-made conundrum pales into insignificance, however, as we confront the omnipotent forces of Nature with these confining beliefs. We now face the greatest threat to our survival as a species, with looming global food and water shortages that, we are told, are only four or five decades away.

The UN made this official in its 2010 (third) Global Biodiversity Outlook warning, in that our Planet's vital signs are failing, adding yet more authenticity to so many other science-based reports.

The pressures upon governments to maintain sound credit ratings, within which to ease the financing of the ever-growing mountains of debt we are creating, will increasingly divert human and financial resources away from tackling this growing natural holocaust that will threaten our very survival.

Current estimates indicate that the time needed to repay global debt runs concurrently with the time it will take for water and food shortages to seriously affect our survival as a species, begging the question – Debt or Food/Water shortages – which gets priority … and who decides?

This desperate scenario is further aggravated by our traditional belief in the financial law of *supply and demand* – the greater the demand for something, the higher its price becomes.

The certain knowledge that global food demand alone could double by 2050 (Source: University of Minnesota. "Current global food production trajectory won't meet 2050 needs." *ScienceDaily*, 19 Jun. 2013), because of a growing population, will cause an escalation in food prices and provide a financial arena in which there are vast profits to be made. Farmland is already becoming an institutional investment, rather than the source of our food supply, as profiteers increasingly indulge in the speculative potentials of this 21st century *gold rush*.

And the picture gets ever blacker when we recognise we have created a double whammy of self-destruction as we now begin to use our food resources as a source of fuel.

> *Leading water scientists predict that we may have to become vegetarians within 40 years to avoid catastrophic shortages of food. 'There will not be enough water available on current croplands to produce food for the expected 9 billion population in 2050 if we follow current trends and changes towards diets common in western nations,' the report by Malik Falkenmark and colleagues at the Stockholm International Water Institute (SIWI) said.*
>
> SOURCE: THE GUARDIAN

As ethanol production increases, so the price of food is increasing and becoming aligned with the price of oil, taking us into uncharted waters where the demand for what fuels our cars directly influences the price we pay for what feeds us.

Once again, we arrive at the same question we had for food/water versus debt – should grain be used for fuel instead of food, or the other way around ... and who decides?

Add to this the pressure mentioned earlier, for governments to choose between feeding their own people and exporting to help pay off debts, and the situation becomes truly mind-numbing.

Our dominating belief in supply and demand can only accelerate the speed with which many are denied basic food and water, as shortages stimulate rising prices that result in only the wealthiest being able to feed and water themselves.

This raises a fundamental question as to whether we have now transformed Life on Earth into an exclusive business club – *Earth Club* – where only the financially capable can survive.

Would it be an act of responsibility on our part to post notices throughout the Planet in all maternity units, and have all affiliated staff carry badges declaring:

WELCOME TO EARTH CLUB
IF YOU CAN PAY – ENJOY
IF YOU CAN'T – GOODBYE!

There is no way we will be capable of overcoming the shortages of food and water that are now looming if we continue with the traditional thinking that has created this dire situation – particularly as we increasingly entrap ourselves in escalating global debt.

This debt, too, has come from troubled beliefs that have seen the largest sector of Society hand vast quantities of money over to a smaller faction, to support their corporate survival. The transfer of so much money from Society is depriving it of the wherewithal to maintain the traditional support systems and services necessary to its healthy running.

I have referred to these beliefs as troubled because I believe they are now threatening the most basic survival needs inherent within us as a species. These needs include the ability to feed, clothe and shelter ourselves and look after the old and sick in the present, and provide education and support for our young.

The most dangerous aspect of what we are now facing ...

The rate and extent by which we are now evolving as a species has meant we have suddenly (in my lifetime) outgrown our traditional codes of moral belief, shaped by Religious beliefs evolved millennia before complex financial instruments, genetic engineering and global governance.

This gap between what we create, and a functioning moral code by which we manage what we create, means we no longer have adequate yardsticks to influence our judgement on what is, and is not, beneficial to our long-term well-being.

At its epicentre is our attitude to warfare and our treatment of human life, something that has dominated human activity since we lived in caves. There was a time, not so long ago, when two armies would come together on a field of battle; both sides being clearly identifiable by their uniforms to mark out the combatants from the civilians in the surrounding area.

Over the intervening years, we have created new weapons of war and methods of warfare that have changed our aggressive behaviour towards each other beyond all recognition.

Today, we rationalise that it is acceptable to *mingle* with the civilian population whilst committing armed aggression, through acts of warfare described as terrorism. Rape has now become a tool of war. And our response to fighting this enemy hidden within the civilian population is by the increasing use of unmanned aircraft – *drones*.

I can see how terrorism has evolved as the only weapon with which to fight a vastly better-equipped adversary, intent upon replacing a traditional way of life with its own political and corporate doctrines. I can also see that drone warfare takes the clearly identifiable soldier out of the range of violent and armed *civilians*. But these evolving beliefs carry serious implications for our future as a species.

> *The relentless march of Western financial beliefs across the Planet 'births' Terrorism, as people with different beliefs and lesser resources strive to resist ... and Terrorism 'births' drone warfare ... leaving only the 'birth' of nuclear aggression!* JTC

If we now hold beliefs that justify warfare within the civilian population, and indeed target civilians to make a strategic point and bring balance to the conflict, then it is only a very, very short step to the introduction of *small* nuclear capabilities.

Inherent within the human condition is a *tit for tat* compulsion when we become aggressive, and it is this fallibility that will take the inevitable step to escalating the size of this nuclear capability until all that remains is a Global landscape that resembles the surface of Mars.

Which *side* discarded traditional moral values to shape the beliefs in how we conduct modern warfare is immaterial. What *is* of vital importance is that there does not appear to be any mechanism capable of hauling us back from the edge of this frightening abyss.

I would, however, contend that a potential way forward is by better understanding and accepting how we function as a species, by recognising our fallibilities and, therefore, the true extent of what we are now doing. Armed with this greater awareness, we can then direct our thinking towards a code of conduct with three basic objectives that:

1. Address who and what we are as a species and how we function.
2. Temper and better manage our fallibilities.
3. Have the capability to evolve with our own development as a species.

I believe a change of direction in our thinking is essential in order for us to survive the current challenges that are a result of our traditional beliefs. Global Magna Carta is NOT a conclusive definition, but a starting point for debate and the catalyst for thinking and beliefs that could take us away from what I believe is almost certain Armageddon.

In order to carry this argument forward, the remainder of this book is devoted to how we might achieve these objectives by examining how we function, what we are all about and the reasoning behind new beliefs that could confront the challenges we now face.

PART 1: HUMANITY …
WHAT WE ARE ALL ABOUT

A Better Understanding of our Most Basic Function

As I look back over my lifetime, I am staggered at just how fast our way of Life has changed, and how little we seem to understand the enormity of what we have achieved.

1. We are able to travel in, and occupy, Space.
2. We are able to communicate directly with each other across the Planet for the first time in our history.
3. We are becoming a Global Village, as modern transportation and technology enable races, colours and creeds from separate countries, states and continents to freely intermingle.

This and every other aspect of Life has come about, not by magic, but because we are a species who create our own destinies and reality through the power of simple thought, belief and the spoken word, driven by an inherent and constant curiosity.

I have seen our minds likened to the soil on this Planet. Invariably, whatever is planted in our mind or in the earth will be returned, but neither cares what is planted.

The soil will grow whatever seeds we plant, be they corn or broccoli, shaping the type of food we eat. Similarly, our minds will grow whatever thoughts are planted in them, creating beliefs that shape how we live Life.

> *We all have passions, interests and abilities for different aspects of Life – we cannot all do everything. There are only so many members of our species who have the drive and abilities to make money, and so many who have the drive and abilities for nursing, teaching, computer programming, or astrophysics, although all are essential in Life.*
>
> *The rich should not be castigated for their abilities. They are simply demonstrating their natural creative talents, in a similar fashion to nurses, teachers and computer programmers. Life is dependent upon ALL of these abilities for us to survive. It is the power we have invested in money and its management that is the problem, and only when we recognise this can we change the parameters for a Life on Planet Earth that truly recognises who and what we are all about.* JTC

With a greater understanding of just how powerful and talented every single one of us actually is, we can change outmoded beliefs that have always held us back from realising our most important quality bar none – *our true potential.* Within that potential lies the ability to create a more sustainable environment in which to live.

Global unification of our species, through the birth of the Internet, is now one of the most fundamental changes taking place. We were once separated races, unable to communicate freely or access each other, without the assistance of institutionalised media and government. Even the thinking behind our traditional religious beliefs kept us separate, and often antagonistic.

It is important for us to recognise that how we treat each other and this Planet comes from beliefs we constructed centuries, or even thousands of years ago. In particular, over the millennia, religious doctrine has impregnated our psyche with the belief that we are born sinners and engulfed in guilt.

Nothing could be farther from the point as far as I am concerned. We are a wonderful species with a myriad of inherent talents, abilities and goodness. If we accept this more positive understanding, we can upgrade our thinking to shape new beliefs that better support, nurture and sustain us through and beyond the advent of our Global Village.

The Single Greatest Cause of all Human Conflict

We identify each other by Race, Colour Creed and Gender. Of all our traditional beliefs, this is the single greatest cause of constant human conflict throughout our history – *by keeping us divided as a species.* In addition, we define each other as *Man or Woman, Black or White, Yellow or Red, Christian, Muslim, Buddhist or Heathen. British, American, African or Chinese* ... the list is endless!

Rich and Poor are added into this potpourri of *labels.* This is probably the most emotive of our current beliefs, whilst at the same time being the most superficial definition of a human being we have ever created. It lacks substance as it fluctuates with the ebb and flow of the financial tides, *promoting and demoting* the credibility of both individuals and groups.

All of these labels imply a difference and, in that difference, either a superiority or inferiority. In truth, our race, colour, creed and gender are simply *overalls* that we enter Life with, covering the multi-faceted aspects that constitute who and what we truly are as human beings. Sadly, we have created and planted belief systems in our minds that convert these *overalls* into *uniforms.* Identifying us as separate factions within one single species has resulted in the few manipulating the many into endless conflicts and abuse to satisfy the fallible human need for power and domination.

From the times of the Roman invasion of Britain, fighting the *Blue savages (the Celts)* through to our more recent history and the barbarism of the slave trade of the 17th century, colour has been the *uniform.* It is by this yardstick alone that we have identified an *inferior* enemy that could be used, abused and waged war upon.

> *Divide and Rule – The Strategy for Power Control of a group of people can be achieved, maintained and increased more easily if factions – or people – are set against each other, inhibiting their ability to unite against the ruler. A prime example of this, in our recent history, was the persecution of the Jews by Adolf Hitler, aiding his rise to power in the 1930s in Germany.* JTC

Inherent within this eternal quest for domination is the traditional and equally spurious belief planted in our minds that each side is in the *Right.* This is a subjective value at the best of times, and open to whatever interpretation justifies and supports the attempted domination of another gender, race, colour, creed or land mass.

When America declared war on Iraq in 2003, the then President stated that 'God was on our side'. He was applying the same battle cry that was used over 1000 years ago when the Crusades were launched by those wearing the *uniforms* of *Christians* against those wearing the *uniforms* of *Muslims.*

These futile wars have caused bloody massacres and destruction through the same battle cry, planted in our minds and continuously repeated over the intervening centuries, with neither *uniform* gaining the permanent domination they seek.

Wars started over political or religious belief, and designed to acquire power through empire, can last many years, and the land ceded can be held for decades or even centuries. However, history shows that all empires eventually crumble, through the dilution of that original belief – *rags to riches to rags in three generations*, is an old but wise adage.

Similarly, the belief in equal rights for women is not a modern phenomenon but goes back to the ancient Greeks, with Plato advocating equality between the sexes in his Republic. Even in the 21st century, women are still differentiated against, in spite of having the same legal rights routinely enjoyed by men.

These *uniforms* that have separated us as a species are now beginning to become rather ragged as multiculturalism exposes the superficiality of this thinking. Increasingly, we recognise that they only identify where we might have resided on this Planet, which country might currently contain our home, or how we interpret our spiritual being.

As human beings, we can never wear just one *uniform*. The truth is, no one adjective, no one name, no one label can possibly identify our many facets. We are not *failures, successes, fat, ugly, losers or stars.* Neither are we our family name – something that can easily change for women with marriage.

Science, too, supports this perspective, confirming that there is no evidence to justify the claim that one race is culturally or psychologically different from any other, or superior (source Wikipedia).

> *When you look at Earth from space, you are immediately in awe of what you see: the incredible beauty of this amazing Planet. It is not until you look more closely that you realise there are no lines partitioning countries or people.* JTC

Add to this modern DNA research, which is of the opinion that we are all from one family whose origins were based in Africa, and it becomes increasingly difficult to support the traditional barriers that have kept us separated for so long.

In the 21st century, the young mix in multi-ethnic school environments, diluting the generations of racial and ethnic conflict traditional thinking has supported. As they discover their similarities with fellow students, they are experiencing the many different aspects that actually unite us as a species.

What are these characteristics the young are recognising, and are they closer to establishing and spearheading the unification of our species?

The Reality that Unites Us as a Single Species

If we ever knew who we truly are, there would be no more wars, no more hunger, no more hatred. We would simply bow down and worship one another.

THOMAS MERTON

As we become familiar with, and more knowledgeable about each other, traditional myths and taboos gradually break down. We are beginning to recognise similar characteristics and traits that are inherent in all of us. This is becoming even more apparent as second generation migrants are born into, adopt and adapt to the language and culture of their parents' new home.

We are beginning to recognise that these inherent characteristics in all of us define more honestly who and what we are as a species. Race, colour, creed and gender are simply refinements that support the different ways in which our collective species experiences Life on Planet Earth.

We are all designed to take up the challenges Life is constantly throwing at us, whatever our situation, making it impossible for any one of us to be more superior/inferior to another.

It is like saying that the different colours in which the same models of a motor car are produced are superior/inferior than others, affecting acceleration or manoeuvrability. Of course, they are not, and it is something we all readily accept.

It is also impossible to apply the *race uniform* to children of a mixed-race couple – they are neither the race of the *white* mother nor that of the *black* father. But all three members of this family have to face the same challenges of work, bringing up a family, education and survival that are also faced by a similar *black* or *white* family.

Each of these three members of the family will have different experiences of the same challenges they all face, uniting them in this thing called Life. Sadly, however, our traditional beliefs keep them separated.

There is no one adjective or noun that can adequately describe the many facets of our make-up as human beings. JTC

If we take a closer look at our underlying similarities, I believe that, by recognising these shared characteristics, we can find a means to our unification as a multicultural society.

Constructing a simple resume can better identify the overriding and indisputable characteristics inherent in all human beings on this Planet. They are the 'engine' within our *overalls* that unite us as a global species.

As an athlete will adapt his or her body to the particular sport they are engaged in, from weightlifter to marathon runner, so we adapt the collective characteristics we *all* share to deal with our individual circumstances and challenges throughout our lives.

Humanity – Our 'CV'

(For the purposes of my argument, I do not think it necessary to try and cover every human characteristic. Also, much of what follows can be applied to the animal kingdom – a subject outside the province of this book.)

Physical attributes

We are split male and female, with common physical characteristics both jointly (legs, arms, torso) and separately (male *penis* and female *vagina* and *breasts*), no matter where in the planet we were born.

We are all comprised of blood, flesh and bone, and are 70% liquid (as is our Planet).

We all have DNA, which is responsible for the transmission of hereditary characteristics from parents to offspring – making every one of us both *the same yet unique.*

We all utilise the powers of verbal and physical communication.

We must process the air, food and water freely provided by our Planet to survive – as well as needing shelter from natural and man-made threats.

We all have family and ancestors, and are both *living* and *dying* during our time on Earth.

We all live and experience the miracle that is Life – we do not need to think about our breathing, heartbeat, or regeneration of our cells. Our muscles expand and contract depending upon usage – eyes see, ears hear – and it's all done without us having to think about any of it.

(Can you imagine what it would be like if it were not? If we had to manage everything our bodies did? We would have no time to do anything else – like reading this book!)

Non-physical attributes

We all have varying levels of personal awareness, which are exhibited and experienced through feelings and emotions – from the joy of laughter, to the overwhelming grief of loss, as well as passions to cavort, create, play and love.

We all have desires to be, do and have at varying levels of intensity that move from apathy to compulsive behaviour.

Driven by our inherent curiosity, we all desire freedom of thought and movement to realise our individual potential. We will react negatively to all forms of repression and suppression when those desires are compromised – although, sometimes, it is necessary for our own good.

This curiosity means we are incessantly restless, as evidenced by our diverse activities across this Planet, from explorers to financiers, and hobbyists to artistes.

We all reason from logical and intuitional perspectives, learning from each other as we journey Life's path.

We all have psychic abilities of clairvoyance, clairaudience and clairsentience to a greater or lesser extent, depending upon our environment and personal awareness.

We are all dealing with internal conflicts arising from previous personal Life experience(s) that shape and colour our individual perspective as we meet with our day-to-day challenges.

Although *Change* is an intrinsic aspect of Life, we all feel threatened and experience fear when it appears to challenge our traditional patterns of thinking and living.

We all have differing perspectives about the many aspects of Life and how we live them. There is an acceptance of female circumcision in some cultures, yet its abhorrence to members of other cultural groups. The staple diet acceptable to some is looked at with that same abhorrence by others.

Empathy and compassion are intrinsic to all of us. When natural disasters hit, it doesn't matter where in the world they occur, we respond collectively with help. Any *uniforms* that separate us are put to one side ... and the greater the suffering, the greater our response.

> *There is something within the human response to suffering which points to a unified understanding that we are 'all members of the same team', up against the common problems that Life can throw at us – acknowledging a deep understanding of who and what we truly are.* JTC

Our aptitude for Life

We all experience the same stages as we progress through Life, from childhood, through adolescence to adulthood, maturity and old age, whether as a Masai warrior, nuclear scientist, or suburban family.

In our 20s, we enjoy our youth, finally accepting we do not have all the answers. We then become more self-assured through our 30s as we leave our previous confusion behind. During this period, we concentrate on crystallising our values and enjoying greater emotional maturity.

In our 40s, we begin to put to use the wisdom accumulated from our growing number of Life experiences, which emboldens our exploration of new territory and attitude to change.

In our 50s, our competitive energy begins to mellow, following adjustments to personal values many make during midlife. As the years progress beyond this point, we experience a sense of greater freedom than ever before, enjoying the growing memories of our individual Life experiences.

We are driven throughout our lives by a constant curiosity that begins in the cradle. This same curiosity makes us fallible as a species, learning by trial and error as we constantly change and create the world about us from what we (or others) plant in our minds.

We also change and adapt to our experiences as we go along, in an Evolutionary process that has been the driving force behind our activity since the dawn of time. This *Intelligence* seems to me to be an *energy* that is pushing us to seek an understanding of our experiences, which will provide us with a deep and lasting peace of mind.

Many of us find personal support by accepting and adopting the wisdom of one of the myriad of definitions of *the presence of a power greater than our own,* whilst the remainder *acknowledge* this presence by rejecting it, no matter how defined.

Of all of our driving forces, the desire to reproduce is the most powerful, ensuring that, *without exception, or priority of race, colour, gender or creed,* we continue as a species to carry out our fundamental task of experiencing Life on Planet Earth in new and diverse ways.

The hurdles we face each day are little different, no matter where we are on this incredible Planet. It is only the refinements of race, colour, creed and gender that affect the same individual challenges every one of us meet. I have also come to the conclusion that there are a *finite* number of challenges we face in Life but, through our *overalls,* we experience them in an *infinite* number of ways.

The need to experience is constantly driving us to create our own reality in a never-ending quest to Evolve. What is planted in our minds that we come to passionately think about and believe in, creates the Life we live and experience, and from which we gather knowledge and understanding.

Our common physical and non-physical attributes, as well as our aptitude for Life, make it is quite impossible for us not to adapt to what we create (e.g. changes in the types of money – from coins to plastic) if it is beneficial to our long-term Evolution. If we are unable to adapt, our current thinking will become obsolete by new thinking and beliefs. It really is that simple and time is always the judge.

Currently, we have created a world based upon financial disciplines, which is now being tested as never before. Time will be the only measure of whether we adapt or grow beyond this present Life we have created.

Can you think of any race, colour, creed or gender across this globe that does not fit within what I have described here?

This constant adaptation and change, driven by curiosity, has been present throughout our history. It defines who and what we are as a species, identifying how we influence our own Evolution, reflected in how we are living Life on Planet Earth at any moment in time. In recent history, this has been identified as the *Industrial Age* and now we are in the process of creating and living the *Technological Age.*

WE ARE, AND ALWAYS HAVE BEEN, A SPECIES OF CREATORS – OF THIS WORLD WE LIVE IN AND THIS THING CALLED LIFE … EVERY SINGLE ONE OF US.

THIS PLANET SUPPORTS AND NURTURES US IN EVERY WAY AS WE CONSTANTLY CREATE AND CHANGE THE ENVIRONMENT IN WHICH WE LIVE BY OUR THOUGHTS, BELIEFS, AND WORDS.

IF SOMETHING WE HAVE CREATED IS SEEN NOT TO BE WORKING FOR OUR BEST POSSIBLE COLLECTIVE BENEFIT, WE CREATE A REPLACEMENT.

THIS IS WHO AND WHAT WE ARE ALL ABOUT AS A SPECIES

> *When we recognise and accept that we all carry the same characteristics within us, we can approach how we live Life from a new direction as we take control of, and better manage, our future.* JTC

Our History Confirms Us as a Species of Creators

Our track record as a species of Creators is truly awesome, as evidenced by each new era we have created. The Stone Age did not end because we ran out of stones, we simply *evolved*. From hunter-gatherers, we moved out of caves and became farmers.

From farming, we moved off the land as a result of our next creation – the Industrial Revolution.

Each stage was not orchestrated by just one individual who then told us all what to do. Although someone first conceived the concept that was adopted in our minds, it took our collective consciousness, understanding and cooperation to create the evolutionary steps that made it all happen.

> *The Stone Age did not finish because we ran out of stones. We simply outgrew it and created a new era!* JTC

It is here that we discover the heart of how we function as a species. This collective consciousness – not orchestrated by any one individual – creates the change in how we live Life. We *collectively* create Life on Planet Earth from a unified thinking, which creates a 'Tipping Point'. (This is covered in more detail at the end of this chapter.)

Farming grew as we saw how we could improve the quality of our lives by creating foraging disciplines that flowed with Nature. Rather than the uncertainties of hunting each day, managing our food supply made it more readily available to us and in quantities that regularly sustained us, dramatically reducing the times when we went hungry.

The Industrial Revolution came about as we realised that we could, once again, improve the quality of our lives by creating and harnessing machinery to do much of the manual work we had previously struggled with.

Not only could we do it more quickly, but also increase our ability to create new, greater visions – expanding our creative abilities, from a wooden bridge spanning a small river to a vast metal cantilever suspension bridge, capable of spanning large estuaries.

> *Some of the greatest ideas of all time have come from people daydreaming, such as Archimedes, Isaac Newton, James Watt.* JTC

Our ability to create a new reality can be seen in the everyday manner in which we have lived our lives over the millennia. From cooking over an open fire, we created kitchens and ovens to manage the heat, thereby improving the quality of the food we eat. Our ingenuity is so great that we have now created the means to cook *without* fire by the miracle of the microwave oven.

We have further enhanced our quality of life by conditioning our food to make it last longer than its natural life – sometimes dramatically so. When the Founding Fathers first crossed to America in sailing ships, some of their food needed to be alive so that they could sustain themselves for the duration of the trip. Even so, scurvy and disease were rife because of the poor nutritional quality of the food and drink.

Gradually, we overcame these deficiencies with spices and, eventually, refrigeration, to prolong the life of our foods. Our creative expertise now has us sustaining the life of our food from days and weeks to months and even years, enabling us to support our longest-ever journeys of discovery as we travel greater distances into Space.

This ability to create, driven by the desire to constantly improve our quality of life, crosses every aspect of how we live Life, from how we travel to how we dress and how we fight each other. Change is the result of the unseen forces of Evolution that power our own inherent curiosity, drive and creative abilities.

> ***We are a species of Creators***
>
> *What we think about, and come to believe in, we can then manifest into physical form. If it works we keep it, until we think of something to replace it. If it doesn't work, we think of something to replace it ... this is Evolution at work!* JTC

What we create and adopt alters Life in such a way as to often make it impossible to sustain the traditional beliefs we previously created. They become outmoded and unworkable, because our own Evolutionary development constantly demands new direction and experience. Our Evolutionary journey is now embracing a new, exciting level of development through the World Wide Web, originally conceived by Sir Tim Berners-Lee. It has been our conscious and collective acceptance of this phenomenon that has led to its manifestation across the globe.

Unlike our previous creations in farming and industrial development, however, the technological revolution is changing our lives at a far more fundamental level. For the first time in our history, we are being united directly and individually with each other – something that has never before been possible.

So dramatic is this new reality we have created that it will drive our personal Evolution in a whole new direction as we share thinking, and implant ideas in each other's minds directly, uncensored by traditional institutions and vested interest.

At the heart of the many challenges we have to face as we evolve and create a Multicultural Society, is the traditional thinking that previously separated us and now needs to adapt in line with our increasing unification as a species. If it doesn't we will leave it behind.

Scientific observations of the 'Tipping Point'

This phenomenon is known in science as *entrainment* and was originated by physicist Christian Huygens in 1666. After noticing two pendulum clocks in rhythm with each other, he became intrigued and set several similar clocks together with randomly swinging pendulums. Within a week, all the pendulums were swinging together, entrained to one another, or in the same rhythm.

Three hundred years later, in 1952 on the island of Koshima, scientists providing wild monkeys with sweet potatoes noticed an 18-month-old female monkey wash the dirt off the food before eating it.

She then taught the trick to her mother, and her playmates also taught it to their mothers as this cultural innovation was gradually taken up. By 1958, all the young monkeys had learnt to wash the potatoes. It was only when youngsters taught their mothers that the practice was taken up. Single adult monkeys continued to eat dirty potatoes.

Then, a phenomenal event took place. As the number of monkeys grew (the exact number is unknown, but let us suppose that one morning the number of monkeys washing potatoes had reached 99 and then the 100th monkey was shown what to do), suddenly, by evening, every monkey in the group was washing the potatoes before eating them.

The energy of the hundredth monkey had somehow created an ideological breakthrough – BUT THIS WAS ONLY THE BEGINNING!

The habit of washing potatoes then jumped the seas as colonies of monkeys on other islands, and a mainland troop at Takasakiyama, began washing *their* potatoes.

This natural phenomenon seems to occur when a certain critical number achieves awareness. This new awareness may be communicated from mind to mind.

Although the exact number may vary, this Hundredth Monkey Phenomenon means that, when only a limited number of people know of a new way, it may remain the conscious property of those people.

But there is a point at which, if only *one* more person tunes in to a new awareness, a field is strengthened so that this awareness is picked up by almost everyone!

(From the book *The Hundredth Monkey* by Ken Keyes, Jr.)

Author's Note

History may bear witness to this phenomenon becoming an integral part of our future way of Life, as its application is supported and accelerated by the use of the Internet.

Different Overalls but the Same Human Energy

When you are next in a busy shopping centre, or any other place that enables you to people watch, just observe without judgement. What you are witnessing are *males* and *females* who are *mothers, fathers, brothers, sisters, sons and daughters.* They are also *shoppers, lovers, homeowners, car owners, worriers, achievers, employers, employees, hobbyists, students and teachers* … at various stages in their lives.

These descriptions define the lives they have created for themselves. And, to complete the picture, there are the more easily identifiable characteristics, many of which they have not had any say in creating. The obvious examples are the colour of their skin, their country of origin, and possibly religious or spiritual beliefs portrayed by their outer appearance.

However, as these fellow members of our species go about their day-to-day activities, they are all living their lives through the same *mind/body/spirit* energy that is inherent within all of us.

From this simple observation, it becomes difficult to understand where all of the conflict and aggression comes from, as we are all basically engaged in the same *job* of living Life.

It is only when we recognise that our traditional beliefs have placed the superficial attributes of race, colour, gender and creed before our universal attributes as a species that we can begin to understand the nature of the problem.

These traditional beliefs have led to separatism, suppression and conflict, all of which were understandable as a less-evolved species. During those times, we were separated by poor transport and even poorer communication facilities, fuelling further suspicion and distrust, born out of ignorance about our superficial differences.

In the new Global Village of this second millennium, these traditional values and perceptions can no longer survive as we grow closer and closer together as a species, dispelling our ignorance and breeding greater understanding and trust.

Of all the observations made throughout this book, this is the most critically important that I wish to make.

> *Only by recognising that we all have the same 'mind/body/spirit within our differing overalls' with which to deal with the challenges Life throws at us with monotonous regularity, do we stand any chance of finding new solutions for the current threats to our future survival.*

We cannot deal with threats of food and water shortages if we are unable to recognise that the problem is the same for all of us. We cannot deal with the challenges of

Globalisation and Multiculturalism if we are unable to recognise that these problems are the same for all of us.

We have now experienced a separatist world and it is something we can no longer sustain or go back to. Evolution will not allow it. Collectively, we are now being driven to create a united world that will support our way out of ALL the challenges our traditional beliefs now present us with.

(I like to define the effects of Evolution as being similar to putting beetroot juice in a moving jug of clear water. The water can never revert to its original clarity ... it is changed forever.)

Recognising how traditional beliefs work against multiculturalism

It was Nelson Mandela who not only recognised the endless problems our traditional beliefs create for us as a species, but the conflict and suffering they have imposed upon us. When apartheid ended in South Africa he diverted the attention of the people away from a seemingly inevitable confrontation by the historic 'uniforms'. He introduced an event that he knew would transcend all of the confrontational issues of that time. That event was 'Sport' in the shape of the 1995 Rugby World Cup final, seen at the outset by experts (wrongly) as an impossible task for the national team to reach or win. During the length of that game, in the stadium and around television sets and radios across the country, the whole nation was united in displaying the fears and exhilaration that identify us as a common species, irrespective of race, colour, gender or creed. Mandela's actions and words reached out and touched the very heart of who and what we are as a species, effectively averting what many had seen as a potential bloodbath. His long period in prison had imbued him with a great wisdom and understanding of humankind that manifested in what history will record as his, and the people of South Africa's, finest hour. JTC

How We Use this Powerful Tool to Create our Reality

From the moment we wake in the morning we create our individual reality from what our mind and body tell us, shaped from our belief and desire to prepare for the new day. Our body tells us to go to the bathroom and *clear and clean.* We then think through our agenda of the day and decide what clothes to wear and what breakfast we need.

We leave the house and decide our means of transport to work. During the day, our mind is telling us how to deal with the myriad of challenges that confront us, whilst our body continues to instruct us to *clear and fill.* We are constantly supported through this work ethic by beliefs that tell us this is the means of our financial support in living our lives.

At the end of the day, we return home and take up whatever hobbies or other interests we enjoy, as evidence of other realities we have created for ourselves and believe in.

Eventually, our body tells us to rest, and so we go to bed and prepare for the new day and all of the new experiences that come from the realities we create in that day.

> *What is now proved was once only imagined.*
>
> WILLIAM BLAKE

It is also important to understand that it is not only our own beliefs and thinking that shape our lives, but also the beliefs and thinking of others that *we allow* to override and dominate our own thinking.

A simple example is popular fashion, covering everything from cars to clothes and furniture to food. Whatever it is, current trends are dictated by the few to the many, although it is still our choice as to whether we adopt their thinking and beliefs, or not.

This same principle applies when we move out onto the Global stage, with such weighty subjects as political or religious belief. In the end, they are thoughts and beliefs that have been promoted by others, and it is up to us whether we choose to adopt them and allow them to be part of our personal lives, or change them for other thinking we find we are more comfortable with.

> *Take a blank sheet of paper. How do we fill it? With words that come from our thinking. From the moment we are born we fill our lives in exactly the same manner.* JTC

Throughout our lives, the world we live in is shaped by the belief systems we adopt, until we are given new evidence and beliefs that obsolete or update previous thinking. Consider, for example, our changing belief over the millennia about Planet Earth and its place in the solar system.

In the beginning, we were told the Earth was flat and if we sailed to the horizon we would fall over the edge. It was Aristotle, in the 4th century BC, who told us that it was an orb. Similarly, for most of recorded history it was assumed that the Earth was the centre of the Universe. In the 16th century, however, Copernicus (a Polish priest with an ability for astronomy) worked out that it was the Sun that was at the centre of our Universe and that our Planet and many others revolved *around it.*

Our beliefs and understanding of the Universe since then have been aided substantially by Dutch lens makers who, in the early 17th century, discovered that, by putting two lenses in a tube, magnification of objects and distances was possible.

At this time it was Galileo, an Italian physicist, who made his own telescope and turned it to the heavens to create a more detailed picture of the Universe, which told us it was not a set of uniform globes.

Fifty years later, Isaac Newton told us that gravity was not restricted to just our Planet but was also responsible for the movement and interaction of all we observe in the night sky. The mathematics he used to establish this thinking now forms much of scientific application today.

What this example also shows quite clearly is how impossible it to sustain traditional thinking when confronted by new evidence, often aided and abetted by new inventions we have created.

We can also see this at work in our own lives. When I was young, the films of the fifties and sixties showed a Society that smoked because it was seen as elegant. Acceptable beliefs we created then played a large part in boosting greater self-esteem and reducing personal tension.

With a new understanding about the harmful effects of smoking, however, the momentum grew to change our mode of living. Today, smoking is reduced to a furtive puff outside of the main social areas of Society. We have created a new world for ourselves, with new methods with which to confront our fallibilities. For many who have successfully given up smoking, including me, any desire to return to the old way has died completely.

> *I have not failed. I've just found 10,000 ways that won't work.*
>
> THOMAS ALVA EDISON

This process of continuous growing awareness of what we are doing, and changing what does not seem to work for our longer-term benefit, is the very essence of who and what we are. We *procreate, recreate, create and un-create* constantly, changing, adapting and updating every aspect of Life as we know it.

From the food we eat, to the cars we drive, and the manner in which we shape our Society's values (traditional Religious belief is now challenged by *Political Correctness* and financial values), we are constantly creating, experiencing, and then changing or adapting Life and how we live it.

We can create whatever we can think up and believe in, that bit is easy. The difficulty comes when the experience of what we have created works against our best interests and the long-term good of the Planet – like cigarette smoking and car emissions.

It is here that integrity comes into play as it becomes necessary to identify *correctly* what it is that is no longer working for our long-term benefit. Only by identifying the problem(s) correctly can we then create effective solutions.

Where the problems have arisen from the dominant thinking we have accepted from vested interests – cigarette manufacturers, for example – the role of effective and honest communication is absolutely critical to the process of finding a remedy. If we are misled with an analysis of what is not working, be it through misinformation, spin or propaganda, we become distressed and distrustful.

As the truth of the need for austerity measures in Greece (and other countries) arrived in the public domain after the financial collapse of 2007/8, increasing unrest at how this truth had been hidden from the people over a period of years actually destabilised the whole population. Integrity is, therefore, essential to the human process and I will return to this subject later.

> *At the heart of finding any solution is the need to correctly identify the problem.* JTC

In the infancy of this new millennium, we are increasingly regulated by the financial values we have created because we believe these values and disciplines enable us to control and value Life. Already, however, we are finding it difficult to adapt to these narrow confines because Life operates from far wider disciplines and values.

Life and our Evolution as a species are unstoppable. The problems we are currently facing from previous thinking may seem daunting, but they also offer an important opportunity for us to recognise what is going on and change that thinking (remember what Einstein had to say).

Above all else, it is the responsibility of every person on this Planet to now recognise that we are just as capable of creating new beliefs to meet our challenges, as we are of staying with the old ones through apathy – the choice is always ours.

> *All we are currently living and experiencing started out as a thought ... every single thing. So start thinking how you want to see and experience the future!* JTC

Human Evolution is Both Relentless and Ruthless

What we think, believe in and speak is the driving force that creates our world. Our curiosity is constantly expanding our awareness and understanding of what is going on around us.

This, in turn, redirects our focus with new thinking that changes the way we live our lives. All of this is happening in a constant and never-ending cycle we call Human Evolution.

If our minds were to become silent, Evolution would come to a halt. That, we know, is impossible, as our best attempt at quelling the activity of our mind is achieved by meditation, and only then for limited periods.

I like to think of the Evolutionary process as like a saucepan of boiling water. When you look at the boiling water, you can see that it is caused by many individual bubbles occurring as the water reacts to the heat. So it is with Evolution, as many individual and group events constantly contribute to our overall development as a species.

I am not sure that we have yet recognised this omnipotent process, as we constantly try to restrict our natural development, often driven by the agenda of vested interest that is motivated by a paradoxical fear of change.

This change is as much a part of our everyday world as eating and sleeping, and is born out of a constantly growing awareness of the world that surrounds us.

If we examine the popular pastime of changing our car for a newer model, we can see this process more clearly and our contribution to it.

Initially, we become increasingly uncomfortable with the look, feel and overall performance of the current model, often as our circumstances change from being single to married and then the advent of a family. The moment we decide upon the type of replacement model, we begin to notice how many of them there are on the road.

In fact, the actual numbers of the new model we now seek that are on the road have not increased. It is our own *awareness/consciousness* of them that has expanded, fuelling our desire to be rid of what we have and to replace it with a new driving experience. We begin to focus on the many new aspects of our desire and how it will improve our current life.

Any criticisms or problems are firmly overcome or ignored if they are preventing our moving forward, unless proven to be insurmountable, like the cost. With all obstacles out of the way (or most of them!) it is just a question of time and effort before the new car arrives on the drive.

If we are prevented from getting the new car, the original discontent still remains until we are finally driven to move in a new direction to satisfy our desire for change.

These emotions are evident in all aspects of how we live our lives. Our homes have evolved from caves, which dictated where we lived, to purpose-made shelters comprising houses and apartment blocks, as we began to *choose* where we wanted to live.

In our relationships, we see how our friendships can change over the years. Often, this can relate directly to personal changes going on inside of us and the resultant new values we adopt (a constant factor in divorce), as well any changes to our personal fortunes during our lifetime.

This continuous drive to create new experiences has seen us develop our abilities to travel, from walking to riding horses, and on to driving cars and flying in aeroplanes.

Our traditional markets, with their individual stalls, and our high street shops, are disappearing to be replaced by vast supermarkets that shield us from the weather and try to meet our every need under one roof.

Our acceptance of homosexuality into the community has accelerated in just the last 25 years, supporting our recognition of the right of people to choose how they live their lives.

To my mind, this major breakthrough in traditional prejudices has also helped Society to release further prejudices about contraception, as we acknowledge the part condoms play in the fight against the 21st century plague that is HIV/AIDS.

Of equally liberating determination is the change occurring as women make an ever more powerful contribution to running Society. I am sure that the Evolutionary process will also be recognised here, and continue to support their tenacity until they attain truly equal status with their male counterparts.

Whilst I have covered a selection of examples that show Evolutionary forces gradually *eroding* the status quo, I am convinced that, the greater our resistance to change, because of vested interests, the more ruthless these forces become.

Never was this more apparent than with the events surrounding the American Civil War. Here, the massive wealth accrued from the use of slavery by the Southern States was seen to be at risk, as a growing voice was raised by the North for the abolition of this odious practice.

Differences became so intense that eventually the Southern States left the Union and created their own Confederacy, resulting in the outbreak of Civil War as President Abraham Lincoln sought to reunite his country.

The war lasted four years (1861–1865) and was the bloodiest in American history. Some historians suggest the loss of Life might have been as high as 750/850,000 killed. When you consider that America lost 400,000 men internationally during World War 2, the loss of life during the Civil War is an indictment of just how intense and savage feelings became about changing the status quo (Source: Wikipedia).

There should be no guilt, blame or shame attached to any of this. The process of Evolutionary change is gradual, relentless and, as we have seen from this last example above, sometimes ruthless ... but always entirely without *judgement.*

This is why we should have no fear regarding our current struggling with our traditional religious beliefs. These beliefs were created by good people and were, of course, relevant to their time. However, our intransigence about beliefs created in the 1st century is straining their credibility as they struggle to support our evolved way of living Life, particularly in Western Society, in this 21st century.

If we are not successful in helping these beliefs to evolve in line with our own personal development, which I sincerely hope they do, then they will be replaced by something else that better supports our current progress.

(Here, it is essential to recognise that the need for spiritual guidance is inherent within every one of us, as evidenced by the many beliefs we are surrounded by, although not always recognised.)

Perhaps a new Pastoral care is already emerging with the exponential growth in the creation of self-help groups to support us in nearly all areas of Life. Here, again, we see our minds creating new directions and realities to experience. Our Evolutionary progress is creating a changing environment in which we are no longer seeking to be told what to do, but rather to become directly involved in supporting each other.

We have become disillusioned with traditional forms of support, both religious and state, as it increasingly appears to be mired in bureaucracy, and intimidated by a culture that now quickly turns to legal dispensation as a means of redress for perceived irresponsibilities.

This disillusionment is further exacerbated by the dramatic erosion of our state services, because of the increasing demands on our financial resources to repay the mountains of debt that have accumulated.

I have always believed that adversity is the breeding ground of opportunity and another facet of the Evolutionary process. Certainly, many self-help groups are practising basic Counselling disciplines, by promoting personal nurture and development through non-judgemental support.

My friend Hayley, a very independent lady, once told me that she wanted to deal directly with 'God', not through somebody else. JTC

In so doing, we are beginning to realise what we are truly capable of working together in this way, bringing out the best in ourselves as a species. This is because this new thinking has moved away from the directing and controlling practices of our traditional institutional beliefs and towards a collective input and management that is more in line with the new disciplines of the Internet.

As we continue to let go of the old and create the new, it is important to understand that there are no *bad* or *naughty* people in all of this. Those who fight the tides of Evolutionary change by desperately trying to hold on to the status quo can either learn from history and concede to this omnipotent force, or be left by the wayside.

Whatever they decide, Evolution will continue its relentless journey into the future, carrying us kicking (and sometimes screaming) along on a ceaseless wave of energy.

I believe the Evolutionary momentum we are currently experiencing in such a myriad of ways (like the bubbles in the boiling water) is yet another aspect that is providing the impetus for us to slowly, but surely, unite as a species. How can we not continue our integration, as our ingenuity creates and expands our Internet technology and new global telecommunications services exponentially?

Add to this the greater sophistication with which we can travel around this beautiful Planet to meet and learn more, both about and from each other, and we begin to realise what a truly powerful force is at work.

Time is also an integral part of the process, and is no protector of the status quo, as we see traditional beliefs that have been in place for centuries, if not millennia, begin to disintegrate. Two or three thousand years is but micro second in the Life of Planet Earth and we need to expand our awareness about this and integrate it into our thinking ... it is the purpose of Life that nothing (except *change* and *words*) should last forever.

With the expanded awareness of the forces at work that are available for us to adopt and manage, comes a whole new level of personal responsibility if we are to truly take charge of our own future. The apathy we have practised in the past, which has allowed the few to impose their beliefs upon the many, has no place in this new world. The decision to go with change is down to the majority and nobody else.

If the gauntlet is taken up, there is still a long way to go and much more to achieve to make us a truly united and balanced Global Society. However, I believe that we have spotted *our new car* and are now driven to make it become a part of our future reality ... but only time will tell.

Words – The Core Power by Which We Create Life

When we look at the centres of power throughout our civilisation, whether it is Governments, Corporations, or Religious Institutions, they all have at their epicentre the means of debate – to exchange words and beliefs.

From the United Nations to the Vatican, from the Houses of Parliament to Microsoft Corporation, there is always an area where people come together to debate the business of their organisation. It can be a boardroom, vast auditoriums such as the European Parliament's semi-circular *debating* chamber, or video conferencing.

Indeed, the power of words, and their ability to create our reality, is always in evidence as decisions and policies that shape our world and our future regularly flow out from these institutions.

Throughout our history, the spoken and written word has always been one of the most powerful energies we can express or indulge in. The spoken word can move us to go beyond our perceived limitations in either direction, whether to build or destroy.

> ***Propaganda is Manipulation by Words and Beliefs***
>
> *Herman Goring was fully aware of the power of words and their ability to manipulate, as was shown in an interview with G.M. Gilbert in 1946 during the Nuremberg Trials. 'The people don't want war. But ... can always be brought to the bidding of the leaders. This is easy. All you have to do is tell them they are being attacked, and denounce the pacifists for lack of patriotism and for exposing the country to danger... It works the same in every country.' See snopes.com*

From this, we can recognise why it is always incumbent upon every one of us, no matter what our position in Society, to be fully aware and responsible for what we say to each other. Its impact is never more obvious than in the messages projected by our media outlets.

In this 21st century, we have become numbed by media hype and political spin as a constant barrage of words assault our senses. Spin and hype are heavily impregnated by the *Right & Wrong* of vested interests, as one side spars with another.

None are designed to create debate for a solid reality, but to win points and try to keep reputations unsullied. Good oratory can inspire, but equally can also become the source of distrust when the words used do not manifest the promised change.

One of our books of ancient wisdom – the Bible – highlights the power of this energy by stating that 'In the beginning was the Word, and the Word was with God, and the Word was God.' The importance of this observation from so long ago cannot be overstated in its relevance as to who and what we are, and how we live and shape our lives.

Nothing bears greater testament to the consistent power words have over us than when Moses brought down the Ten Commandments. The construction of these words had a fundamental impact upon how we have conducted ourselves as a species right up to the present day – we accept it as a crime, anywhere in the world, to kill or abuse each other.

Calendar-makers are aware of the power of words and often carry a *Daily Inspiration* – words constructed in such a way as to cause us to think each day about Life and our present place in it, often influencing or reassuring us with illuminating insight or nagging questions.

Poetry throughout the ages has held us to account in its clever use of words, as it opens our eyes and hearts to the wonders of Life, as well as its mysteries. Our advertising industry concentrates solely upon words to emphasise images that portray messages designed to influence our perception of our Life and how we might change and improve it.

As words create the Life we live, throughout history we have looked to those people who have had the best oratory skills and methods of conveying them to lead us.

From Shakespeare's portrayal of Mark Anthony's speech at Caesar's burial, to the 2008 US Presidential election directed at millions of people, we have been transfixed by the visions good orators have painted with their exemplary use of words.

> *The two most engaging powers of an author are to make new things familiar and familiar things new.*
>
> SAMUEL JOHNSON

Taken to its extreme, we experienced the last World War open and close through thinking and beliefs that were brought to reality by the words of both Adolf Hitler and Winston Churchill.

At the end of the First World War, Germany suffered what was perceived by many as a humiliating defeat, and proved the breeding ground for Hitler's beliefs. From this defeat, his oratory built a new belief within the German people about their place in the world. This same oratory and powerful beliefs then took Germany into another conflict that escalated into the Second World War.

In Britain, Winston Churchill had been suspicious of Hitler's beliefs and motives and was subsequently proved correct. His own unflinching beliefs in the ability of the British people to deal with this overwhelming threat manifested in his oratory skills and world-renowned speeches, as his country gradually became isolated by the German advance across Europe.

History is witness to the eventual outcome of the war and the power of one dominating belief over another. The cause of this bloody conflict and its ending, as well as the support of the Allied forces responsible for Hitler's ultimate defeat, could not have happened if it was not for the powerful words sown in the minds of all the people involved throughout its course.

> *Do not say a little in many words, but a great deal in a few.*
>
> PYTHAGORAS

In the corporate world, discussion by the board of directors may reach a decision that a new product is needed. Researchers are briefed and they ask the public questions. Their replies form the basis of the reports the research company submit back to the board.

If the report is implemented and the product created, the marketing departments create advertising materials, both written and spoken, that endeavour to sow seeds in their customers' minds that their new product will provide them with a better life than the one they currently have.

This whole process is fuelled by what is thought and believed in. From the initial board decision, through the research, marketing and sales, it is what is created by words that underpin the physical objects (the products). Our decision to buy, or not, will then contribute to how we live our Life.

The creation of this book you are now reading demonstrates this principle. What I thought about and came to believe in was transformed into the written word that is presented in this book. The book could not have come into being without the thought and belief to begin with. This is the very essence of our true power as a species of Creators.

Whilst words create our individual reality, there is also another powerful and exciting dynamic at work that can convert our individual thinking into radical change in the wider world we live in.

This is how our political environment has functioned for millennia. We are all aware of how the people who seek election endeavour, successfully or not, to stimulate our thinking to support what they are advocating.

A tipping point is reached when they get enough like-minded people to support their entering government and the same process plays out when they seek election to positions of leadership.

As I understand it, tipping points are incredibly easy to achieve. Only 7% of the population needs to become aware of a new idea – whatever that may be – for it to become a household word.

Evolutionary change, in the shape of our Global Village, is now applying this phenomenon with greater intensity. Driven by the capabilities of our Internet technology, we are now creating ever more tipping points within this new environment as we send our own thoughts and creations around the Planet in milliseconds.

Indeed, we have a new phrase to identify this exciting event, when what we create or think goes *viral!* The most obvious example of this is with the first published work by the author E L James, *50 Shades of Grey,* astounding everyone by its global acceptance and placing her work in the Best Sellers lists for all of 2012.

If you accept that our lives are created by what we think and create, then Life on this Planet is now changing forever.

> *I do not agree with a word that you say, but I will defend to the death your right to say it.*
>
> VOLTAIRE

No longer are we restricted to the thoughts, beliefs and words of the few to shape our lives. This new global environment is encouraging all of us to now speak out and decide what we want out of Life, opening a whole new chapter in our Evolutionary journey through the uncharted waters of Life.

Right & Wrong ... Words that Constantly Mislead Us

Whether changing our car or finding a new relationship, building a business or championing a cause that is special to us, feeling *comfortable* with what we are doing is essential to our journey through Life.

Each experience we create is driven by our own thinking and personal desires, and will nearly always attract comment from our fellow Life travellers, intrigued by whatever direction we are taking.

What we create can either make others feel comfortable and supportive, or uncomfortable and therefore critical. This often manifests in *judgement* as they declare that what we have created is either *Right* or *Wrong*, from their own perspective.

If words are at the centre of this process, then it is here that we arrive at the greatest abuse of their power. *Right & Wrong* do not define whether something has failed or not, but rather sidesteps this critical process in an endeavour to intimidate.

When others judge what we have created to be *Wrong*, they will endeavour to ignore, change, suppress or dismantle our work. In the worst case scenarios, where negative feelings become intense, they can result in repetitive conflict and war in an effort to control or subvert our activities – inevitably, vested interest is driving this subversion.

Here, we strike at one of the central aspects of how we live Life on Planet Earth, as we endeavour to change and control what others create and believe. At its most extreme, our history is witness to our attempts at global control of our primary beliefs, from *Crusades/Jihad, Capitalism/Communism, The Final Solution* and many others, all with causes proclaimed as *Right*.

Needless to say, the passionate and repeated cries of *Right & Wrong* from vested interests have not resulted in any single belief coming out on top. Indeed, all that has been achieved is constant conflict within our species resulting in the loss of innocent human life in stupefying numbers over the millennia.

Wars are fought over political beliefs, religious beliefs, racial beliefs and corporate need for raw materials. This is because vested interest dictates they are always in the *Right*.

Our preoccupation with vested interest is at the heart of our inability to coordinate a strategy, as a species, that will better manage the resources of our Planet. As fast as we agree a global plan of action we renege on it, in whole or in part, because of the pressures and interplay of vested interests.

It is *Right* to counter the effects of global warming; it is *Right* to maintain profit growth for the sake of shareholders; it is *Right* to restrict our tree felling of the Amazon rainforest; it is *Right* to create employment for those clearing the trees as it provides them with food, clothing and shelter … the list is endless.

Our preoccupation with what appears to be a rational point for each vested interest continues at the cost, in this example, of establishing a responsible stewardship of our Planet for our future survival. Until we address this problem, we will never effectively manage this beautiful Planet for our long-term good as we continue its unremitting plunder.

> *'Right & Wrong/Good & Bad' push us to one side, or leave us struggling in the wash of the ship of vested interest. 'What works & doesn't work guide her safely through the minefields of Power & Greed.* JTC

As the interplay of vested interest endlessly bounces back and forth, it is a truly amazing spectacle of verbal ingenuity, if it were not for the fact that the lack of an end result to all this activity is taking us to our own self destruction. *Right & Wrong* just doesn't work!

However, I am confident that our frustration at the inability to create a better reality from the tangled web of *Right & Wrong* will eventually lead us into the clear-sighted boundless arena of *What works* and *What doesn't work* in our best interest as a species. The latter value is an integral part of the natural Evolutionary process and, therefore, intimately linked to who and what we are.

There is no better subject with which to make this point than with challenges we have wrestled with as a species over the Religious beliefs we have created (how unsettled we can become by what others believe in). So much so that, over the millennia, there has been a constant drive to not just override one single belief, but to *dominate all of them* – because our belief is Just and True … and *Right.*

I have stated before, I believe it is generally accepted that, at the heart of the human condition, there is a *spiritual* essence which manifests in a variety of ways, including *Buddha nature,* which is similar to what is called *Christ consciousness* in Christianity, the *breath of God* in Judaism, and *higher consciousness* or the *life force* in Humanism, and its presence is identified in its very denial by atheism!

> *When every religion states that the members of all other religions are doomed to go to 'hell' – then surely, by the very nature of this general diktat, we are ALL destined to go to 'hell'!* JTC

We can see that Islam works for a Muslim and does not work for a Christian. Of fundamental importance, however, is the fact that, through our differing *uniforms,* we are nourishing the *same* tool within us all.

As we come together in a Global Society, it becomes essential for us to recognise this need for deeper understanding that is prevalent in every member of our species. We share and enjoy each other's food, but are incapable of enjoying another's religious beliefs, perhaps in the latter case because power can be derived from this aspect of how we interact.

When religion is as enjoyable as food, we will have achieved true mutual respect and understanding, ending forever the *Rights* and *Wrongs* that have kept us apart for too long.

I would go further and suggest that the growing horror of global terrorism can never be resolved by our traditional institutions, because it is their separatist *Right & Wrong* thinking and beliefs that has contributed to it.

If we continue to confront this threat with dominant military thinking, whose beliefs pursue *victory over the enemy*, we risk constant global warfare, and history shows there is never a winner to this. In addition, increasing levels of personal surveillance and data holding will destroy the healthy functioning of a free democracy, making the supposed cure worse than the suffering.

Only when people come together with a better understanding and acceptance of their differences will the *Right & Wrong* of terrorism become less credible. Letting go of judgement and the need to dominate is replaced by a desire to cooperate and contribute in creating a greater respect for each other and our many diverse means of living on this Planet.

Once we can recognise that *Right & Wrong* do not work and get us nowhere in ending human misery, we take charge of our destiny, opening up to our true potential for unconditional human interaction and creativity the like of which we have never experienced before.

We Cannot Survive as a Species Without Integrity

If you accept that we are constantly creating and experiencing Life on Planet Earth, then of equal importance to us is our ability to accurately assess what we create and experience.

It is only by doing this that we can see what is working and what is not working in the best interests of this Planet and its Inhabitants and whether it is in our longer-term benefit to continue with it, change it, adapt to it, or ditch it. After all, *we are the only players in this thing called Life.*

I firmly believe that a sense of integrity is deeply entrenched within every one of us and a fundamental part of who and what we are as a species. I would go even further and say that integrity is as essential to our healthy functioning as the very air we breathe.

If integrity is such an essential part of us and the means by which we can precisely assess what we create and experience, surely it is supporting and guiding our Evolutionary journey as a species and emphasising the point to our being here?

We acknowledge the importance of integrity in Life by placing our judicial system at the pinnacle of our Society, as one of its most powerful and respected institutions. At its very core is the drive to establish the truth, by deciding upon the validity of the words used during a trial, or any other judicial session. Any attempt to hide, or in any way interfere with this process carries severe penalties.

It is worth noting that the tenacious and much respected QC, Baroness Kennedy of the Shaws, and for whom I have the greatest of admiration, best sums up the impact of the law on Society in her book Just Law, where she defines it as "the bedrock of a nation". Certainly there is little else that has impacted our lives in a similar fashion and defined how we conduct our relationships with each other over the centuries.

There are times when the process falters through human fallibility and results in miscarriages of justice. However, these failings do not in any way threaten the credibility of a system that, in large part, meets our overwhelming desire for integrity, and our need to place truth and honesty above all else in human and planetary interaction.

I would also put psychotherapy, in its many guises, alongside our judicial system as another process that works to help us to find the truth about what we are unaware of, or avoiding, within ourselves.

The healing qualities and sense of release from personal stress achieved by this practice can be overwhelming, as we recognise the unsullied truth about problems that have affected our happiness, perhaps for decades. It is the recognition of this truth and honesty about past events in our lives that can then provide us with an invaluable reassurance about Life and our place in it.

However, our interactions with each other can often function without integrity, breaking bonds of common trust that have caused us unremitting pain and hardship over the millennia.

At its most simple, I am sure that many of you, like me, have purchased something online and parted with money, only then to experience the non-appearance of the goods. Trust is immediately destroyed through a lack of integrity by the seller, prompting us to anger, frustration and vowing never to return to that site again.

Trust and integrity are such vitally important aspects of how we function that, in this instance, we introduced *purchaser ratings audits.* These audits are becoming common now in our pursuit of integrity, seeking to identify just how honest and efficient these services are from the experiences of users.

Here, sellers who are not acting in integrity are brought to task, either by the host site banning them, or their potential customers simply walking away because of poor ratings. The lesson being that, whenever we step outside of integrity with each other, we create problems, both large and small which, if not addressed quickly and honestly, can sometimes become insurmountable through that loss of trust.

> *In a world where more and more information is held about us, I am indebted to James Slattery-Kavanagh for making me aware of the discipline of Data Fading. If this discipline were made a requirement of all who use the internet, my understanding is that data requested and given up for specific purposes could only be held for a limited period before being destroyed, or the specific details made more general i.e. instead of full postal address the neighbourhood or city only would be retained. This discipline not only mirrors the workings of the Natural world, in that nothing is hoarded because everything gets broken down, but would dramatically increase our trust in giving up personal information, as well as equally dramatically reducing the opportunities for abuse.* JTC

When we move into the world at large, we can see just how inextricably entwined both trust and integrity are in every facet of our lives and how critically dependent we are upon them.

When we drink water, we trust in the integrity of the natural streams and rivers, or the man-made devices and reservoirs, not to poison us.

As drivers or pedestrians using any means of transport, we trust in the integrity of the people who make the brakes and steering wheels that they will not fail and harm us, although accidents do happen.

Another (glaringly) obvious example is with people who rock climb, as they place their lives in the hands of the integrity of the harness and line-makers who supply their safety equipment.

When we write to someone, either by snail mail or email, we trust in the integrity of the service provider to deliver our messages to their destinations. The same is true of our food suppliers, and there is uproar when tainted food is found in the supply chain.

Here, our dependency on integrity is related to tangible items that we can see and touch. However, this trust in honesty and integrity is tested exponentially when we venture into the arena of the global belief systems we create.

The very use of the term *'belief system'* shows us it is demanding our trust in following the words and beliefs of others. With nothing tangible to examine, our trust can be extended to the limits of our patience after we have given it.

The passing of time is the only means by which we can prove that these beliefs were honestly presented to us and are working in our best interests. When the beliefs, particularly of vested interest, are seen not to be working for the common good, serious problems begin to manifest.

Because time is the means by which we assess the integrity of these beliefs, it too can also work against us, because the Evolutionary process is constantly changing our surroundings and how we view Life. The longer any beliefs remain unchanged in a constantly changing environment, the greater the challenges upon their validity and integrity.

Integrity and Religion

Of all human activity, Religious belief is a uniquely creative process across our species. What is conceived, believed in and spoken about can only create something intangible.

At the heart of this belief is the desire to bring relief from suffering as we make our journey through Life. It is only at the most personal level that we can make a decision as to whether these beliefs are doing their job, by assessing their contribution to our overall feeling of well-being. This is no mean task, as our well-being is often severely tested as it fluctuates in line with the ups and downs of our daily life

These fluctuations demand an act of *faith* by us towards those who have created and expound the beliefs they are sure will bring us support and well-being. Faith is the highest level of integrity we can offer as Creators.

For thousands of years, we have committed to a myriad of beliefs supporting religious or spiritual conviction. The strength of this faith has been constantly demonstrated when we have laid down our lives in defence of our particular beliefs.

However, time has produced flaws in some of the beliefs and rituals that have demanded this high level of integrity from us. This, coupled with a growing multiculturalist society, is calling the dominant *separatist* traditional thinking of these institutions into question.

What has previously been portrayed as unquestionable divinity at work is now seen as great wisdom interpreted by vested interest and managed by human fallibility, as traditional institutions resist the march of human Evolution.

The significance of this for us as a species could not be more devastating, because it is these traditional religious beliefs that have underpinned our moral codes. From business to politics and how we conduct ourselves within Society, traditional religious creeds have set the benchmark for our conduct.

The challenges upon our religious institutions to provide succour from ancient beliefs, which try to address the stresses and strains of our modern world, are now becoming increasingly obvious as congregations continue to dwindle in Western culture. If our well-being is not nurtured by existing religious belief, then we will eventually walk away and create something new to replace it.

Integrity and the corporate world

All beliefs are dependent upon our trust and nothing is truer than with our financial thinking. Whilst we have tangible evidence of the presence of money, and the constantly evolving methods in how we use it, the *value* of that money and the new methods of using it are taken very much on a trust in the integrity of our financial institutions.

Here, time is playing its part as yet another financial collapse in 2007/8, and the methods being used to remedy it, are seeing us question whether this belief system is truly working in our best interests and those of the Planet.

There is no doubt, from both the experts and those forced to assume ever-mounting levels of personal and sovereign debt, that we are becoming enslaved to a monetary system that offers no apparent reprieve or support.

> *A lack of regulation has fuelled a disregard for integrity in all we do. Lack of integrity breeds lack of trust, which is now apparent across the very institutions we have created to manage Life on Planet Earth, paralysing our ability to remedy*

the problem. Indeed, it was the father of modern economics, Adam Smith, who said that 'trust is higher in fair societies'. JTC

Since the crisis of 2007/8, due in part to the lack of transparency and integrity of those involved, not even the most sophisticated financier or databank has any idea of how much *bad* debt is now contained within the global system.

This problem is further exacerbated because of the manner in which the complex financial devices that caused the problem have been packaged and distributed. It, therefore, follows that nobody has any idea of just how much *good* money needs to be put into the this system to remedy the problem.

It is rather like trying to erect a large hotel on quicksand. Where is the firm ground, and how much concrete will be required to create a solid foundation on which to build the hotel?

If ever there was proof of the catastrophic effects of ignoring integrity it is here, and we need to seriously take this on board as a species. I believe it is necessary to stand back and look at what motivated this loss of integrity, and set in place the means by which it can never happen again – covering up is not an option.

It could be argued that, as this debt has come about by methods and practices that have lacked integrity, those who have become the victims are fully within their rights to show a similar lack of integrity and renege upon its repayment, ensuring some form of deterrent against future reoccurrence.

Whilst this could be seen by some as an attractive option, I question what sort of moral landscape this would leave us with, where trust could be irreconcilably broken down across our species.

From our own personal experiences, we know that, if we lend money, no matter whether to our family, a friend or business partner, if our trust in that person has been misplaced we will forever remain sceptical about repeating that gesture again. It stigmatises the relationship and, like virginity, cannot be returned once lost.

We are all responsible for the World we live in. There are no good or bad people, only human fallibility. The bankers lent the money and we took it. The Greek people are to be respected for accepting their part in their country's crisis and both Wall Street and Greek politicians might learn from this and bring new thinking to heal the problem. JTC

Driven by greed, the need for trust was completely ignored by many, as it became obvious what huge profits could be made from trading in the *sub-prime* derivatives market, as one trader sought to outdo another. The vast amounts of money made from these nefarious dealings is now quite useless in trying to repair the trust that has been destroyed across the global banking community, something that has been an integral part of their business dealings in the past.

This mistrust has permeated out into Society at large, as mind-blowing amounts of money are being printed and pumped back into the banking system in exchange for these toxic assets. Although originally justified as the means by which money could be injected into the economy to stimulate demand, the banks have held on to this new money, stimulating one gentleman I overheard in a coffee bar to suggest that it has become the biggest money-laundering exercise in our history.

All of this pales into insignificance in my mind, however, compared with the effects this could have upon future business because of this erosion in trust between bankers. Could it see Society waiting in a kind of financial limbo, over perhaps a decade or more, whilst trust is repaired, or worse, until a new fraternity of bankers and institutions pass up through the system that are once again able to fully trust each other?

I don't know, but I do know that we are at a different level of Evolution as a species now, and the world is a different place to that when the last financial catastrophe occurred in the 1930s.

I would suggest that our traditional financial system is now being challenged because we are outgrowing it. Certainly, the protests are gaining momentum across the globe, as the young, in particular, react against the imposition of debt repayment for something they had no hand in creating. In this terrible environment, where do we begin to restore trust?

> *Subtlety may deceive you; integrity never will.*
>
> OLIVER CROMWELL

Again, I am unsure. But, if it is to be decades before the present financial system is able to function as efficiently as it previously did, then what are our options? This is something I will return to in more detail in the next section.

Integrity and politics

If we now turn to political beliefs, these, like religious belief, trade on words and ideas. Time once again is an integral part of the process, as government is all about the beliefs that directly shape the environment in which Society functions, and the trust we place in those beliefs to deliver what is promised.

'In this world nothing can be said to be certain, except death and taxes' as Benjamin Franklin said in 1789. This humorous quotation belies the vast responsibility that is at the heart of any government, as it undertakes the supervision of the money we hand over to support the services needed in the running of Society ... and the century's old resentment by Society to handing that money over!

I don't for one minute believe we are not happy with the concept of Society paying for the services it uses and needs. I think that, at the heart of the problem, is the constant abuse of trust that has occurred by successive governments in how they *manage* that money.

In the infancy of this 21st century, credibility and trust is now being seriously eroded within Western Society, because of the growing gaps in the provision of all of our public services, due primarily to our living longer as a species and an expanding population, all of which is exacerbated by the financial crisis.

These problems have not suddenly occurred during one electoral period, but have been evident for decades by successive governments in many countries. It is here that mistrust has grown as these same successive governments have pushed these issues to the bottom of the pile, to become 'problems for the next government'.

If we then add to this the misuse of the taxpayer's money, without mandate from the taxpayer, to rescue the institutions responsible for the recent financial collapse, it is not difficult to understand why a belief in any political party to now take us forward has been hopelessly undermined.

In the UK, we have seen the *Expenses scandal* that highlighted the abuse of public money by representatives in both the House of Lords and Parliament. Here, sometimes substantial amounts of money designed to cover the expenses of those involved in carrying out their public duties were diverted through false expense claims for their own personal use and benefit.

In the EU, whilst it is accepted that their budget is vast, for nearly two decades now auditors have been unable to account for sizeable amounts of taxpayer money.

From both of these examples, we can see how hard-earnt taxpayer money is being treated with, at best, irresponsibility and, at worst, with absolute contempt. Here, human fallibility is blinding those involved to the long-term damage these situations are causing to the credibility of the tax system.

Integrity: The mortar securing the bricks in the 'Mansion of Society'. JTC

I believe that at the heart of these unfortunate situations are political and corporate actions that are no longer underpinned by traditional religious beliefs, which previously held sway over our moral conduct, thereby rocking the very foundations of Western culture.

A 2010 poll conducted by the Pew Research Centre in America centred on electors' trust in government and showed that only 22% of the respondents trust the government all of the time. Sadly, there has been a steady decline in trust in the government over there since 1953, when the Eisenhower administration enjoyed a trust factor of over 70%.

To my mind, this lowering of trust is indicative of what Carl Jung referred to as the *collective unconscious* at work. Something deep within us detects that the spoken word is not representative of political thought and action.

This lost trust is not because people were *bad* or *naughty*, but because human fallibility, in the shape of vested interest, has driven them to words and actions that do not reflect the true situation. Hence, our current ignorance about the scale of toxic debt within a broken financial system and, equally, broken health, pensions and education systems – broken not by their own functions, but human fallibility.

> *I never did, or countenanced, in public life, a single act inconsistent with the strictest good faith; having never believed there was one code of morality for a public, and another for a private man.*
>
> THOMAS JEFFERSON, 1809

Honesty and truth are a responsibility we all carry to our fellow inhabitants of this Planet as an integral part of the Evolutionary process. History continues to repeat itself with monotonous regularity as we hide behind the fallacy that ignoring integrity doesn't matter. What we do know, however, is that when we ignore it, events will always come back to bite us ... and bite us hard!

> *Integrity is a fundamental aspect of who and what we are – we cannot survive as a species without it.* JTC

Integrity and the 99%

When we identify the perceived personal failings of those in the public eye, a highly-prized sport by media publisher and reader alike, it would be irresponsible to ignore the similar failings in Society at large.

The tragic death of Princess Diana in a high-speed car chase was the result of a culmination of circumstances prevalent in our Society today.

Photographers, driven by the lure of huge fees, were aggressively seeking pictures of her. Newspapers were eager to print these photos because they were guaranteed a readership, whose thirst for such material was proving insatiable. This, in turn, made the papers large amounts of money from advertisers, eager to get to those readers.

The similarities between the relentless chase after this beautiful woman and foxhunting seems a little too close for comfort. Hypocrisy dictates that we condemn one and allow the other to flourish unabated.

When we are able to accept our collective part in her death, we will then be ready to seek out thinking that helps us to moderate our excesses. Maybe the huge outpouring of grief at the time was a subconscious display of that acceptance and desire.

What is worryingly evident now is that the circumstances which eventually led to Diana's death continue to be played out by some sectors of the media. Sadly, this is now aided and abetted by the explosion into the public arena of *phone hacking*, as they compete with each other in a frenzy of flashing lights and new technology for that all-important headline.

This behaviour is unpardonable and has to be bought under control, by addressing the moral ethics that allow it to flourish, if Society is to continue to have investigative journalism providing the backbone of an essential and healthy democratic process, something I shall return to again later.

In our lust for personal gratification, be it from power or greed, our loss of desire to assume responsibility for how we treat each other and manage our surroundings will eventually result in our own destruction. The tsunamis, hurricanes and other planetary *vibrations* are getting worse, not better, as we continue to rape the Planet and each other in our blind pursuit of financial nirvana.

> *It is easier to cope with a bad conscience than a bad reputation.*
>
> FRIEDRICH NIETZSCHE

Living our lives with integrity becomes more demanding than ever as we gradually integrate into a truly Global Society. Given that there is no turning back from this Evolutionary step, we need to find the courage to practise the honesty we believe to be true about who and what we are.

There is no greater challenge upon us now than to assess the social, political and religious beliefs that have influenced us for millennia, and their place in this new and dramatically changing climate.

Only with an acceptance of the role of integrity in our lives can we begin to grow *respect*, the most quintessential and all-important factor in uniting and supporting our Global Multicultural Society in its efforts to begin managing the Evolutionary process for the first time in history.

PART 2: CREATING A NEW WORLD OUT OF THE OLD

The Evolution of Money

In the Beginning ...

I find the whole subject of how we have adapted to differing means of exchange with each other over the millennia as yet another perfect example of our working in unison with the Evolutionary process. We create the new and discard the old with an ingenuity that is really quite breathtaking. Throughout this process and into the future, money, in its many guises, is only ever a function of trust ... no more, no less.

In the beginning we created barter

I had firewood I had collected from travelling the surrounding area during the day. My neighbour had a deer he had caught that same day.

I could not be bothered to hunt for food after a day getting wood, and he could not be bothered to search for firewood. Therefore, we swapped some of what we had for our mutual benefit – a cooked meal that evening.

Then we created specie money

Barter was fine but, as we accumulated more possessions, it became cumbersome to drag them around with us. Shells and then coins are what we next created to cut down on the quantity of goods involved in bartering with our neighbours.

The problem with money was that, like barter, you needed to carry more and more of it around as your wealth grew – and the likelihood of robbery increased.

Then we created fiat money

Our specie money was backed by a tangible asset which, in the case of coins, was the metal they were made from, while notes could be redeemable for gold.

Fiat money, on the other hand, is not backed by a tangible asset but by government decree that it is legal tender. Legalising the tender provides government assurance that it will not become valueless.

Then we created Plastic money

Great! No more weighty wallets showing evidence of our wealth. A little card does everything barter and money had done before, but without the need for coins, notes or a cheque book.

Even this means of payment is being expanded, as retailers join with Google and big cell phone companies to offer payment systems that utilise mobile devices as sophisticated *interactive plastic*. Who knows where this will take us as we evolve a whole new breed of payment methods.

And now we are creating truly Digital money

We are constantly expanding the capabilities of our new technology, and nowhere is this truer than in helping us manage our need to trade. This is becoming more evident with the increasing use of mobile phone technology and *Internet Money* that no longer require coins, notes, cheque books, credit/debit cards ... or Banks!

We are already using Internet phone services like Skype to talk to each other through our computers and mobile devices around the Planet, and at little or no cost. In a similar fashion, we are now seeing *digital currency* being exchanged by those same computers.

Sites such as www.bitcoin.org offer the software and, like the phone services, there are little or no charges. Like Skype, this is also a direct service between users who have absolute control over all their transactions. The increasing popularity of this service is evident in the value of the currency, which rose by 500% in 2012. Not only that but we have now seen the introduction of their first ATM in Vancouver, Canada in 2013. In Australia they can now be used to purchase the all-terrain Tomcar vehicle ... and this is just the beginning!

Will there come a time when we create our own personal currency, managed by our own personal integrity and financial standing? Who knows, but what I am certain of is that we are now being united as a species by Evolution, and that it is an unpredictable bedfellow!

So far so good, but I believe there have been some aspects of what we have created along this Evolutionary path that are constantly challenging both the human condition and human fallibility ...

Profit – The Compulsive Element to Money

Throughout our history, we have had a love/hate relationship with money, and in particular any income we make from its use – be it profit or interest. As far back as Ancient Greece, Aristotle declared his hostility to usury, an attitude reflected by the teachings of both the Qur'an and the Bible, which have influenced our reservations about 'money making money' right up to the present day.

Whereas the proceeds from a Lottery win come from our collective contributions and most of it is shared out among many, profit and interest also come from our collective contributions but are accumulated by the few, and then shared out to the few.

Since Christ threw the money lenders out of the temple two millennia ago, those institutions responsible for our moral well-being have confronted this subject in a constant ebb and flow of intensity. That the subject does not go away indicates to me something deep within our collective psyche that says we are uncomfortable with some of our derivations of money and how we accumulate it.

At this level, we seem to be aware of how its intrinsic characteristics can stimulate our fallibilities, as demonstrated by both our vulnerability to greed, and the lengths of abject humility we will descend to in order to acquire it, neither of which lead to anything other than grief and misery.

At the dawning of this 21st century, we find that the derivatives of money we have created have brought us to our knees. This has been caused by greed and lack of integrity, once again, and surely point to our need for a strong new moral direction to be created and constantly applied for our future collective safety and wellbeing.

This can only be successfully achieved, in my opinion, by better understanding who and what we are, and the recognition and acceptance of our fallibilities as a species. JTC

When we moved from bartering with goods to 'bartering' with money, the benefits of the exchange became blurred. We could see how much firewood we needed to cook the deer and how much deer we needed to feed ourselves, making it easy to trade with each other to satisfy our needs.

When we created money, we introduced a *whole new can of worms* into the business of trading, without realising it. This *money* we had created was useless in directly feeding, clothing and sheltering us, but it could be hoarded for as long as we wanted, unlike the natural resources we need to survive, which deteriorate over time.

Because it was not an *essential* commodity like the wood and food we had previously bartered with, it was difficult to work out what it was actually worth. This complication meant that an intangible value was placed upon a shell/coin, which could then be traded for tangible items such as a cow/sheep/water/clothing etc.

It is here that human nature then took over. The individual with money sought to transfer as few useless coins as possible, in return for as many essential life-sustaining goods as possible. In that moment, *profit* was born.

The spurious nature of this value has ignited human fallibility to greed ever since, creating a belief system that promotes making larger and larger amounts of profit with seemingly no ceiling.

Although this belief in making profit has remained unchanged throughout the millennia, its increasing dominance in directing how we live our lives is systematically degrading the importance, quality and value of the very commodities we need for our survival.

Chickens, for example, have lost their status as inhabitants of this Planet and become *units in a factory battery process*, which denies them any right to grow and develop naturally. This process appears to be constantly reducing their nutritional contribution to our healthy functioning in the cause of profit – something touched upon earlier.

However, it does illustrate the point I am trying to make about the precarious risks to Society, and its health in this instance, because of the overriding importance we place upon the dominant need for endless profit.

If you accept that compulsive behaviour is a fallible human condition, I believe that when we created profit we activated the compulsive qualities within money.

After all, the poppy is a beautiful flower, but becomes a powerful drug when transformed into opium and heroin. Grain and grape are harmless and nutritious foods until transformed into whisky, wine and brandy.

The effect of compulsion upon human behaviour is well-known, manifesting in a fixation for the *high* provided by whatever commodity, or other illusion-producing activity (e.g. sex), has attracted us.

Profit stimulates the compulsive impulses of greed within the process of trade, as we strive for that big fix of *something for nothing.*

> *Madness is badness of spirit, when one seeks profit from all sources.*
>
> ARISTOTLE

The primary symptoms of compulsion, I would suggest, include:

a) *Obsessive behaviour* – A single focus on the fix, and little else.

b) *Irresponsible behaviour* – A fix at whatever cost.

c) *Compulsive behaviour* – Constantly repeating actions and behaviour known to be detrimental, or of high risk.

d) *Denial* – That a), b) and c) above are not the case.

In the pursuit of profit, a couple of hundred years ago Britain became Great on the back of the slave trade. Here, the tantalising myth of *something for nothing* – captive human beings – induced scant regard for the misery this pursuit of profit caused.

Justification for those actions can, in part, be derived from our makeup as hunter/gatherers, and the need to fulfil the basic human drive for both achievement and survival.

However, the excitement that came from hunting for food was tempered by the fact that there was little benefit in gathering more than we needed, because the excess rotted back into the ground. The greater the excess, the greater the waste.

On the other hand, we can gather and *hoard* limitless amounts of profit. This subtle, but important, difference to our gathering instincts for survival seems to me to stimulate the compulsive forces within us.

The effect of Profit upon Society

The other subtle, negative influence within the constant drive for greater levels of profit is that it separates us from each other. The sheer scale of modern business organisations forces them to detach from the intimate interaction with the community that was possible when small businesses dominated the high street.

> ***Master Or Servant To Our Impulses***
>
> *A Spiritual Master watches as one of his students passes his meagre food ration to another student in return for a cigarette.*
>
> *'You will never become master of your Life until you conquer your own fallibilities,' comments the Master.*
>
> *A year later, the student approaches the Master and confides that he has not had a cigarette since their conversation. The master smiles, pulls out a pack of cigarettes and offers the student one.*
>
> *(A story my father told me many years ago).* JTC

These traditional family businesses built *goodwill* with their customers, bringing people together in a manner that can still be observed today in the remaining small local shops. This was a uniting factor that created awareness of the local community, as well as a sense of belonging.

We enjoy personal interaction as a species, whether social or professional, and this has been lost as we move our shopping habits from small shops to out of town supermarkets and shopping malls.

The natural interaction from a personal service that helped us reach an informed decision about our purchases has been superseded by our lonely vigil down endless aisles, where our senses and decision-making faculties are assaulted by price alone.

The belief that we are getting cheap food is a myth of monumental proportions, as the subsidies we have to pay farmers to produce this 'cheap' food come from the taxes we pay, reflecting the true cost of what we eat and drink.

We have created vast emporiums that no longer build goodwill, but rather buy it with *loyalty schemes* that drive us to spend as much money as is possible in support of the bottom line.

Our ingenuity has helped us to understand all there is to know about how our impulsive behaviour manifests when shopping, and how to stimulate those aspects to maximum advantage in the pursuit of profit.

This has resulted in our being inducted into our newest 21st century *uniform* as a *consumer* (rather than a customer requiring a service), joining all of the many other *uniforms* we are identified by, that contrive to separate us rather than unite us.

> *Forty years ago, I bought my parents a small fridge, which I kept after they died. It is still working very efficiently now and the door seal is as perfect as when I bought it. I cannot think of any modern household good that would last as long.*
>
> JTC

With present business models geared to endless profit growth, the corporate mission is vertically driven and has become a *profit* machine. Intense focus is placed upon constantly lowering production costs by keeping wages low and materials as cheap as possible.

Products no longer remain as functional for as long as they used to, as people are constantly bombarded with the newest must-have model – mobile phones and football shirts stand out here. With this sort of pressure, what spare earnings are available to explore all that Life has to offer, should we choose to seek them out?

> *The drive for profit has seen us create such efficient fishing fleets that we are indiscriminately taking from the seas supplies that are beyond our immediate needs, and in ever growing quantities that must eventually inhibit the Planet's ability to replenish what we take out.* JTC

We are already seeing large corporations merging into vast global entities, which are at greater risk to abuse of power through our limitations as human beings. In recent times, we have seen these global entities manipulating the banking LIBOR rate, which affects millions of people with mortgages, for example, as human fallibility seeks to further enhance profits.

(It was widely reported that the collapse of Barings Bank, the oldest bank in the world, was because the senior directors did not fully understand the risks inherent with the financial instruments that were making such vast profits ... until after it all collapsed!)

Underwriting this level of human fallibility under the banner of *Too big to fail* is a duty the taxpayer of the 21st century may not continue to see as a *social* responsibility. As lender of last resort, their lack of reward when providing this service willingly, or unwillingly, is a type of enslavement that will surely become untenable.

This unhealthy situation is further aggravated by encouraging the vigorous pursuit of profits and the inherent high risk involved, in the certain knowledge that, whatever mistakes are made, the financial support will always be there to restore the company to good order once again.

What we have not yet become aware of is that, endemic within all of this vigorous activity, is the Evolutionary process at work. Be it corporations, political empires or any other aspect of our activities, they eventually collapse through excessive over-development and greed ... and with monotonous regularity.

Profit and the Natural Cycle

In business, the underlying process is called the *product life cycle*, which follows four stages – Introduction/Growth/Maturity/Decline – and mirrors the same progression followed by Nature. We know that, when growth is accelerated, be it plants or businesses, they become difficult to sustain, increasing the likelihood of them toppling over.

Whilst our ingenuity, as always, is to be applauded, these techniques have serious implications for our long-term welfare. This same ingenuity is increasingly taking from our Planet far more than we actually need, be it 'fish or fowl', unbalancing the natural order in Life by inhibiting the Planet's ability to naturally replenish these stocks.

We stockpile vast quantities of fish, for example, in freezers and tins designed to extend natural life spans in the interests of reducing stock wastage and improving profit margins.

Our technological achievements cannot be faulted. Indeed, I would be the first again to applaud human ingenuity, were it not for the fact that we are pursuing a course of action that is dramatically and fundamentally flawed. Vast though they are, the resources of Planet Earth are *limited* and were never designed to support our drive for *unlimited* profit growth.

The thinking behind this same profit growth also insists that costs have to be held to a minimum, which is understandable. One of the biggest costs for businesses is the wage roll and so, in this new global environment, corporations are constantly searching out and moving their operations to those countries that have the lowest wage structures. However, the reality of this thinking is that we now have an environment in which workers across the Planet are permanently enslaved to low wages.

Redefining Profit

If our Planet's limited resources cannot support constant profit growth, and growing social unrest will not support constant low wages, it seems to me there are two ways forward. Firstly, it may become necessary for governments to impose a charge for the use of their employees, national resources and infrastructures. This would certainly allow countries to catch up with the tax avoidance practices companies are now (legally) capable of in a new global era that is still practising traditional taxation beliefs.

Secondly, and of greater preference to me, is to take up a more positive challenge that could see future business expansion determined by corporations turning inwards and recognising the compulsive properties of profit. It might then be possible for an expansion of the present business model, to supplement financial profit growth with *human* profit growth, bringing a broader base to current business activity.

This would herald a marked change to our traditional beliefs about the dominance of profit. In an environment such as this, corporations would continue to be encouraged to make as much money as they can, whilst also respecting the dignity of this beautiful Planet and its inhabitants by returning a lot of that money to the sources from whence it came.

There would be a quantum expansion in the recognition and place of Corporations within Society as they would no longer be defined solely by the amount of financial profit made. Instead, they would be defined by how much was made *and returned* to employees and suppliers and the Planet, in addition to shareholders.

> *Labor is prior to, and independent of capital. Capital is only the fruit of labor, and could never have existed if Labor had not first existed. Labor is superior to capital, and deserves much higher consideration.*
>
> ABRAHAM LINCOLN

Current narrow beliefs supporting the drive to maximise profit seem somehow self-defeating to me. Corporations rely on consumers and governments to purchase their wares, whilst striving desperately to hold down the amount of money they return to those people and bodies in wages and taxes.

It seems to my untutored mind that they should be doing the opposite, by returning as much as they can to support their future business. This is how it works in Nature, with everything being returned to the originator – the soil – and I've yet to hear of Nature going bust ... although, we are currently stretching matters with our plethora of abuses.

The effect of recognising our current narrow thinking and widening those beliefs as described previously would be like adding water to whisky – diluting the potency of the compulsive qualities of the alcohol (profit) without spoiling its enjoyment.

With a wider definition of what constitutes corporate *profit*, corporations would have broader goals with which to challenge the ingenuity of management in the pursuit of that broader *profit requirement.*

With this new focus on corporate achievement, a dip in the profit activity of the company is less likely to stimulate a frenzy of panic and fear. In the present climate of compulsion to profit, a drop in profits from £200 million to £50 million sends stock markets into apoplexy because of the constant and unrelenting pressures to outstrip the last set of financial results.

What is overlooked in the current intensely restricted environment is that £50 million is still an awful lot of money – even £50 of profit shows the company is trading soundly.

> *'Competition' between businesses is centred upon the creation of profits, instead of how we evolve the employees and customers. Simply changing this thinking would change the rules of engagement and the face of modern Society.* JTC

Many businesses have operated successfully for decades, and even centuries, and it is not business practice that I am now questioning but the intensity of the business environment. No one can question the fact that it has steadily become more pressurised through the demand for profits from aggressive Stock Market behaviour.

The belief that a free market can self-correct is only possible when all the players have a deep understanding, acceptance and respect for who and what we are and how we function as a species. Any regulation that is deemed necessary will reflect the gap between this understanding and actual market practice.

It is this additional and increasingly intense pressure for profits by the financial markets that, as with any other form of compulsive behaviour, breeds sharp practice that leads to mistrust, as new ways are sought to support bigger and bigger profit fixes to keep shareholders and markets continually satisfied.

(To this end, businesses are coming under increasing pressure not to provide badly needed jobs to the growing numbers of unemployed people in the interest of maximising profits. The moral dimensions of this action are not the province of this book, but highlight compulsive thinking that is in serious conflict with its desire for consumerism as the lynchpin to its recovery.)

> *As evolving human beings, we seek to experience Life in its many guises. If we are discouraged from pursuits because they are not financially advantageous, we limit our true purpose and potential as a species.* JTC

The traditional thinking that created the problem is now trying to resolve it. Sadly, therefore, the situation can only get worse. Talk of expanding current regulation is not the cure to compulsive behaviour – it never has been.

Recognising the cause, however, goes some way to addressing the problem by focussing more closely on how to manage human fallibility, whilst also fulfilling our most basic of needs as hunter gatherers.

Whatever the outcome, you can be sure of one thing: if current social unrest expands, we will create something to replace the single-minded drive for profit and that will be very exciting indeed.

Credit Seems to Work Against the Human Condition

Today, we have created a piece of plastic which enables us to use other people's money to buy anything, from a take-away meal to a yacht – and we don't have to explain or justify what we are using the money for.

Our ingenuity has become more and more sophisticated as we move inexorably towards a paperless Society. Electronic media and *holes in the wall* allow us to generate money, be it our own or someone else's, with the application of a numerical signature ... *money on tap!*

The ease with which we can access this financial resource has become increasingly more adept. Tales abound of people holding between six and thirty different pieces of plastic, enabling them to create mountains of personal debt in their pursuit of an illusory happiness that inevitably leads to personal misery.

This raises the question as to whether this belief in credit is healthy for us as a species. To me, it seems to directly oppose the fundamental human condition.

I have come to the understanding that human beings are designed for *effort and reward.* This simple principle is inherent in every aspect of our lives, from physical fitness to material wealth, and from artistic to academic endeavour.

Only by making and experiencing some effort towards what we seek are we able to also experience a sense of reward and personal benefit in the achievement. (A famous author once stated that she 'didn't enjoy writing, but *having written*!')

> *Credit is a system whereby a person who can't pay gets another person who can't pay to guarantee that he can pay.*
>
> CHARLES DICKENS

This is why competition is such an essential part of our Life experience. Competition drives us to achieve *the prize,* whatever this may be – a possession, an award, or recognition.

It is this effort that is also the motivating force behind the respect given to us by other people when we attain our goals. We all recognise when someone else has struggled to achieve, and the evidence of their commitment somehow resonates with us at a deeper level.

Ellen MacArthur DBE held the world enthralled by her remarkable achievement in 2005. Not only did she sail around the globe single-handed, but also set a new world record for the time taken.

This, and numerous other personal achievements, is the embodiment of what we are all about and how we function at our best. This human characteristic also highlights other important aspects about how we function.

> *The greater the difficulty, the more glory in surmounting it. Skilful pilots gain their reputation from storms and tempests.*
>
> EPICTETUS

If we look at our relationship with money, I would like to offer this personal experience. As a kid I had a money box into which I paid my weekly pocket money, supplemented at Christmas and birthdays by gifts. It was always exciting to open the box and count its contents, as the kitty built up towards that something *special* I wanted to buy.

I remember saving up to buy a toy train from the local toy shop. Whenever I went past the shop, I would look in the window to make sure it was still there. The day finally came when I had enough money to go and buy the train.

The excitement and sense of achievement was overwhelming. I came out of the shop with my prize and played, looked after and cherished it for a long time.

This story attempts to illustrate the human condition at work in not only manifesting a desire for the toy, but also a *depth of commitment* to attaining that desire. The weekly saving was a source of personal achievement and satisfaction because of that commitment.

(At this time, the British currency was pegged to the gold standard and the price of the toy remained static, providing an underlying stability to the whole process.)

> *We have now learned that rashness and imprudence will not be deterred from taking credit; let us try whether fraud and avarice may be more easily restrained from giving it.*
>
> SAMUEL JOHNSON

Credit, on the other hand, enables us to buy something without any effort, and then spend months or years striving to pay for it. Invariably, the item we crave and buy loses its appeal quite quickly, because the actual striving comes *after* the achievement. What starts out as a positive experience eventually becomes stressful and unrewarding.

This, I am convinced, is caused by a subtle shift in our attitude to attaining what we want, from commitment to *impulse*. Commitment identifies a deeper sense of need, whereas impulse reacts to a much shallower sense of craving that identifies our compulsive behaviour.

This impulsive action is further supported by modern plastic cards which transfer our money *invisibly*, posing new considerations that were never an issue with hard cash. All credit transactions become transfers of *numbers* from one account to another, with little sense of *physical* loss or movement.

The sense of loss that I somehow feel, when taking cash out of my wallet, is simply not present when dealing in plastic. I believe this subtle change represents another of the many challenges facing human beings in this new technological era we have created.

Credit supports a belief in consumerism which, in turn, challenges our sense of self-worth because of a limited sense of personal achievement from this highly impulsive activity. As with anything impulsive, it becomes necessary for us to constantly repeat the *shopping fix* with an accompanying spiral of accumulating debt, as we to try to buy our way out of our constant struggle with self-esteem.

It is here that we can see the compulsive qualities of unregulated credit following a similar pattern to profit in its effect on the human condition. This time, however, it affects the majority of people rather than the few.

We are still smarting from the credit card frenzy of the 1990s and early years of the 21st century, together with our subsequent enslavement to the mountains of debt created from our impulsive behaviour.

Mortgage credit, on the other hand, supports the human condition by providing the means by which to secure our shelter from the elements and also in which to bring up a family. Here, we are able to apply tighter definition and regulation to the purpose for which the money is to be used, for example a house or flat, taking away the impulsive element that plastic encourages.

If we can recognise and accept our innate drive to achieve through striving and accomplishment, as well as our fallibility to human impulse, then perhaps this might be the foundation upon which we rebuild our relationship with credit.

It is only when we can recreate *revolving* credit (plastic) in a form that can work with and support the human condition that we will restore confidence in its currently dented image.

> *Nothing so cements and holds together all the parts of a society as faith or credit, which can never be kept up unless men are under some force or necessity of honestly paying what they owe to one another.*
>
> CICERO

All of this also begs the question as to whether we are capable of adapting to the new psychology *digital* trade demands, with the movement of numbers rather than cash. Time alone will be the judge, but what is certain is that either we will adapt, or create something new to replace it.

Managing our Lives by Financial Disciplines

We have created a series of beliefs that increasingly encourage us to live our lives by financial disciplines, effectively reducing our ability to actually live and experience Life through all of our faculties, as fully integrated human beings.

This is the effect of the Evolutionary process we are currently going through and therefore asks the perennial question ... when these disciplines appear to come into increasing conflict with who and what we are as a species, is this because we are not adapting to them, or do we need to change something?

As money is the means by which we interact through trade with each other, should it not be our servant rather than the master it seems to have become at the beginning of this 21st century?

> *Capitalism seems to entail growing debt for it to work. Even when standards of living were supposedly improving, this improvement seemed to be supported by increasing debt. If this belief is dependent upon the majority spending money to support the system, it would appear that people do not have enough of their own money to make it work, necessitating the need for them to use other people's money (debt) in increasing amounts.*
>
> *It is a system that is doomed to failure unless more money can be provided to the people who need to spend it, without recourse to the volumes of debt that bring the whole edifice crashing down. This is, to me, the central flaw to the thinking that has created this belief. Profits are hoarded instead of being recycled as higher wages to the consumers to 'refuel' the system, thus allowing it to flourish for the benefit of all.*
>
> *The flaw in hoarding has been evident since the financial collapse of 2007/8, when the biggest tranche of global money in our history was taken away from the mass of the people and placed in the hands of only a few. Whilst satisfying the need to hoard is an integral part of our Capitalist belief system, there is now less money available to spend in supporting the process.*
>
> *And the bow wave of this hoarding is played out in cities like Detroit and elsewhere across the globe, where homeless families live under bridges and walk past countless empty houses that used to be their homes. Here, our current financial thinking actually comes between people and their basic human right to live on this planet and be protected from the elements.* JTC

Whilst money has occupied our attention for millennia, it is now becoming such a dominant part of how we live Life that it is competing with the most basic of natural functions within Society.

Our personal integrity is now measured through the narrow perspective of how we manage our money, and particularly the money we borrow. This limited definition is applied by potential employers as well as educational establishments, particularly in the West.

I find it worrying that our ability to repay debt seems to be of higher value in assessing our character than the ability to learn, or interact responsibly with each other in the numerous other ways in which we are capable.

A credit rating tells nothing about a person other than his or her attitude to, and ability with, finance. It tells nothing about their human attributes of care, compassion and integrity, her or his concern for those around them, nor their ambitions and goals in Life.

> *We limit our experience of Life when we allow any single belief system – be it Religious, Corporate, Social or Political – to dominate how we think and act.*
> JTC

We are now increasingly measuring our daily lives by financial criteria, seemingly to bring some sort of meaning to each experience. News programmes will automatically carry the financial implications for most of the stories they cover, something that hardly ever occurred when I was young.

The concern for those suffering tragic Life events used to be the story, not the potential subsequent cost to business or government. Human tragedy is an integral part of Life, but it seems as though our dominating financial beliefs now make it essential to include any financial implications associated with a tragic event, to further dramatise it as well as bring meaning to the story.

This, in turn, begs the question as to whether limiting our appreciation of Life to purely financial considerations is now constricting our ability to access our compassion, and fully appreciate and understand the many other aspects that make up the world around us.

We are increasingly turning to the Stock Market when a tsunami or similar catastrophe occurs to identify how we should be reacting. If the Dow falls, fear spreads out into a Society that seems unable to recognise this is purely a financial reaction, and has no bearing whatsoever on our continuing ability to feed and clothe ourselves.

The food, clothing and means of shelter provided by this Planet can never be taken away from us, and this should always be our dominating belief when assessing the catastrophes and other events that are constantly going on around us.

These financial beliefs are exploding exponentially across our species, now affecting the way of Life of two of our largest countries – India and China.

It is exhilarating to watch as people increasingly realise their natural potential, with young entrepreneurs now building businesses that had not been possible for them to do only a few short decades ago. However, one cannot help wondering if the debt problems currently faced by Western countries will soon blight these mighty continents.

> *Freedom of the markets is only possible if there is a strong moral code that directs the ethics within those markets.* JTC

As we look deeper into the problems we are now facing, we should ask ourselves the question: did they begin when we no longer linked the true value of money directly to this Planet and its resources, such as gold? Whilst I reiterate that I am not an economist, something deep inside me tells me that, once we broke this link, we allowed human fallibility greater sway in managing the substance of this commodity.

Instead of linking our borrowing capacity to the assets we held, which could then be sold if we got into trouble, like any other financial transaction, we moved away from what we owned and began borrowing against what we *thought* we could repay.

Whilst I am sure there are those who would argue that tying money to the gold standard inhibited our ability to freely develop its potential, I would counter argue that it is for this very reason that we now have mountains of debt.

(It was the father of modern economics, Adam Smith, who warned against the pitfalls of fiat currencies unpegged to anything real. He also called for a ban on high-risk, high-interest lending, the 18th century version of subprime.)

It is also the reason for the mind-numbing problems now being experienced by the people of Greece and other countries. These situations highlight the need to better understand who and what we are and how we function.

We are fallible as a species, deliberately so in my opinion, as part of the *Life Experience.* When it comes to the management of money, surely it would be wiser to tie its market value to the availability of natural tangible assets, recognising this fallibility within us.

> *Adequate regulation, through recognising our fallibilities, would have prevented every financial crisis we have experienced over the centuries.* JTC

To this end, I wonder whether the gold standard itself was flawed because it tied us to just one commodity. Life is about contrast and variety. By expanding beyond gold and into silver, diamonds and copper, for example, we not only spread the ability to value our money, but also place a 'democracy' behind its valuation. After all, is it not a fundamental aspect of a *balanced* investment strategy that we spread our activity across varying sectors of the market?

There is another facet of Capitalism that suggests we are now creating means by which to extend the use of money beyond its simple face value, and into uncharted waters that warrant greater understanding of where we are going, or trying to go.

Our acceptance of debt and leverage means that *money is growing ever larger in quantity, but in the hands of a reducing number of people* who understand the greater complexities of the instruments we are creating for its use.

If this trend continues, and there is no reason to doubt this, then presumably we reach a point where, eventually, all the money in the world becomes the sole possession of one person, to whom the remainder on the Planet become indebted.

Ok, let's hold our hands up and cede victory to the disciplines of Capitalism and the process of accumulation. The *experts* have won – now what?

History teaches us that there are Universal Disciplines at work in all areas of Life, and they will never allow dominance of one belief of Life over everything else – it upsets natural balance, another Universal Discipline. Every attempt at world domination by one facet of Life – be it political, corporate or religious – has always failed and will continue to do so.

I have alluded earlier to aspects of our financial beliefs that work against the Natural order. Here, it is probably the right place to highlight one of the more serious infringements of this omnipotent process.

In Nature, all animals nurture their young and then *push them out of the nest* when they are old enough to look after themselves. We have now created a financial environment which actually inhibits this natural process. The implications of this, to me, are frightening. Our young are no longer able to *leave the nest* as we and our parents used to. Our current beliefs have seen our young take on unprecedented levels of debt for their age. These same beliefs are also responsible for rising rental and purchase prices of potential homes.

Just these two aspects of modern-day Capitalism are now making it increasingly difficult for our young to follow the Natural order and begin homes of their own – at a time when their body clocks are telling them they should be.

> *America's sophisticated financial system was once seen as a pillar of economic success, but Wall Street has since become synonymous with greed and irresponsibility in the public mind. Is free and unregulated market innovation really in our collective best interest?* JTC

By inhibiting this basic function, we are playing with forces far greater than we appreciate – the very forces that define and influence what Life is all about in our world.

Never before in our history have there been such restrictions to living Life as those imposed by the current financial beliefs now being experienced by our young. I am sure this has a lot to do with the riots now playing out in many parts of the world, and speaks of a collective consciousness that is now awakening.

Our past is littered with slavery of one form or another, and those who overrode them. What history teaches us, from the fall of the Roman Empire to the conflict in present-day Syria, is that oppression always ends in revolution and upheaval as the overbearing status quo that is no longer working is replaced by something else.

I believe that the current dominating financial disciplines will once again see history repeating itself as we respond to this modern form of enslavement by debt. I fear, however, that the consequences this time will be without precedent in this nuclear age, as the world splits itself into two frenzied groups once again, one seeking to change and the other fiercely holding on to the status quo.

> *We are even now questioning whether the end of 'cheap food' is in sight – a sure sign that present financial thinking is not only dominant but also threatening our very survival.* JTC

If we add to this the certainty that Capitalism cannot survive the Natural forces of climate change within the current model, then rising prices from reducing resources can only ensure a conflict between the rich and poor, thus accelerating the onset of global nuclear war, as I have said before.

Having said all of this, I would offer that, by searching out those aspects of Capitalism which support the effective management of this Planet and our lives, we can create new thinking and beliefs that work in harmony with the Natural order. In so doing, we might discover a new respect for the adaptability of this financial discipline in a rapidly changing world.

> *A final perspective on Capitalism. As I watched a blackbird singing in the garden this morning, I thought how happy and contented he sounded with his uncomplicated Life. But maybe he was laughing at us – as we ponder whether our grandchildren will be able to continue to repay the mountains of debt we are currently building, and that increasing numbers of us will be in poverty through failed pension provision. Money has no place in his Life, and it rules ours – maybe there is a mid-point!* JTC

The Money Supply and the Laws of Nature

A little history

It was the Knights Templar who introduced the humble beginnings of our modern banking system. This Order was the brainchild of a French knight, Hugues de Payne who, in 1119, with the support of King Baldwin II of Jerusalem, sought to protect Christian pilgrims with a police force as they travelled the bandit-ridden countryside to the Holy Land.

The success of this policing service was fine-tuned in 1150 when the Order created *letters of credit* for the pilgrims. This enabled them to deposit their valuables at one Templar fort, travel to the Holy Land, and there be reimbursed using this piece of paper as evidence of their deposit with the Templars.

Several centuries later, with the abolition of the Knights Templar by a debt-ridden Pope, the goldsmiths took up a similar service. This time, the safety offered for the gold and valuables were not forts and armies of heavily-armed fighting men, but very strong safes.

This simple procedure, of issuing pieces of paper as evidence of safely stored valuables, which could subsequently be redeemed, is the forerunner of our cheque books and international banking system today. Over the centuries this process has expanded into an infrastructure that transports money to every nook and cranny of our Planet.

In providing this service, the early goldsmiths discovered that the valuables deposited with them were often left for long periods of time and that only a part of their deposit was normally required by the owners, the remainder sitting idle in the vaults.

This idle money *deposited* with them provided the goldsmiths with the means to create a secondary business by putting it to work as loans, earning income from the interest and fees they charged for this additional service.

By recognising that only a small part of the money they handled would need to be held in *reserve* to meet the immediate needs of the few, the Reserve banking system was born and remains in use as our dominating financial belief system today.

Whereas the goldsmiths lent out the idle money they held, the bankers have turned this process on its head by lending out more money than they have assets to cover this money, knowing that only a fraction of it will ever be immediately called upon.

This financial system is entirely dependent upon confidence in the banking system for it to function effectively. History is witness to this loss of confidence at work when all of a bank's depositors demand the immediate return of their money and, of course, the money is not there. We see rumour of insolvency turn into a *run* on a bank, leading to its eventual collapse and the loss of credibility by depositors and the public at large.

This was at the heart of the credit crunch in 2007/8, when money lent out to *sub-prime* mortgage borrowers saw them eventually, and predictably, become incapable of meeting their repayments. The numbers were so great that the property market collapsed, leaving banks with little or nothing of value to sell to get their loans back.

They became insolvent and so the money they needed to fill the hole in their accounts from unwise banking practice was taken from taxpayers in an endeavour to make them solvent again. Only time will tell whether this strategy works, or not.

Having said that, the ingenuity with which the financial industry has driven their disciplines and beliefs into such a dominating position is to be admired.

The money supply from Private Banks

For centuries they have managed the most basic of our needs to trade with one another and, unlike our religious beliefs, they have mirrored their banking practices to the changes brought about by our own Evolution as a species. With the advent of the digital age, our notes and coins are gradually converting into *digits* that we move about on our computer screens, or with pieces of plastic that use the bank's computers.

How our money comes into being is a task that is very much the province of the *private* banking sector in the West. Over the centuries, private banks have come to provide the supply of money instead of the government, arguing that the creation of money should be kept apart from potential abuses by the political system.

Indeed, money is the business of banks and so it is not unreasonable for them to provide the expertise. They are also private commercial companies and, therefore, it is equally not unreasonable for them to seek profit from this activity. This profit comes from interest and fees, as we have already established, and so all money provided to Society comes in the form of debt.

Private banking organisations, such as the Bank of England or the Federal Reserve in America, print money which is then supplied to private banks at low interest rates. Those banks then use that money to buy government bonds, which pay interest on those purchases.

Looked at from another perspective, these bonds are like credit agreements with the banks, where the government undertakes to repay the money to the banks at some time in the future, or when the banks choose to sell the bonds. In the meantime, the governments pay interest to the banks for the use of this money.

The government then distributes this money out into Society in the shape of payment for government contracts, social benefits and a myriad of other functions. The money received from the banks is never actually repaid because, obviously, if it were there would be no money available for Society to use.

When these transactions occur, only enough money is put into circulation to meet the needs of the government and there is no surplus with which to meet the interest payments to the banks. More money is then issued for this purpose and interest is again payable.

Over time, issuing money as debt will see the interest payments grow considerably. This is because the original money from the banks is never repaid and compound interest (the common practice of payment of interest on the interest, as well as the loan) escalates the debt the longer the money remains unpaid.

Over 10 years, an original loan of $1000 would increase to between $6000 and over $7000 depending upon when the interest is paid – monthly, quarterly or yearly (Source: Wikipedia). The longer the loan term, the faster the debt grows. $10,000 at 6% compound interest grows to over $180,000 after 45 years. (Adapted from *Web of Debt* by Ellen Brown)

> *An analogy for the money supply from private banks. It is like lending our children their pocket money and charging them interest on it. They can use it for whatever purpose, whilst paying the interest, which we would also lend to them. As their only source of income, they cannot repay it as they would then be without any money. Looked at from another perspective, if they did repay it they would have to borrow it back again.* JTC

If we go back to the origins of barter, we traded known Planetary items with values we could easily access – the wood for the deer. Traditionally, money's quantifiable value was linked to gold, maintaining its links with easily accessible Planetary resources.

During this time, prices remained stable. Indeed, I can remember my father telling me that is was common practice for couples to get married and save for their own home, which they would pay cash for in their middle age because prices were so stable.

However, financial thinking suggested that holding money supply to a Planetary resource, such as gold, was holding back our development and so, in the 1970s,

President Nixon took the American dollar off the Gold Standard and turned it into fiat money. What this means is that he legalised the production of the American dollar without its capability to convert back into gold, a decision that has been the subject of controversy ever since!

Where gold stood guarantee for the value of money before 1971, it is now underwritten by government assurance that its value can be supported by government resource, rather than Planetary resource.

This led to the wide-scale printing of money, as credit was encouraged to improve our quality of Life. Certainly, it has produced more home and car-owners, together with a greater number of young enjoying higher education and families living fuller lives. Sadly, this has all been achieved, as I have said before, not by releasing us from the gold standard, but from growing debt and the interest that this debt accrues.

If we then add to this a vastly expanding money supply, *Quantitive Easing,* that has come into being following the financial crisis of 2007/8, there is seemingly no limit to the amount of money that can be printed and the subsequent interest that has to be paid.

The flaw in fiat money is intriguing, as it actually works against the very financial beliefs it was designed to support. The law of supply and demand dictates that, when something is in short supply, its value goes up because of demand. Conversely, when something is plentiful its value falls. This is what has been happening to fiat money over the decades, as more and more of it has been printed and entered the global money supply.

This is what inflation is all about. The cost of our planetary resources and what we do with them is constantly increasing, because the value of our money keeps falling. As more and more of it is printed and supplied as debt, further amounts then need to be printed to pay the interest on that debt.

The need to constantly supply additional money to meet the interest payments for the money placed in circulation has the effect of increasing the cost of our Planetary resources which, paradoxically, remain the same. A house is still bricks and tiles and wood – whilst the value of the English pound has dropped by 85% since the 1970s (and the American dollar by 88% in purchasing power since 1950).

In 1969, when I first got married, you could buy a three-bedroom house for approximately £2500. That same house today costs £250,000. This illustrates how our confidence in money is eroding; as growing quantities of it are printed to meet the interest we have to pay on the money in circulation, making it impossible for its value to be held steady.

The money supply from Public Banks

Whilst there is a strong argument for allowing the private companies to supply and manage our money, I can't help feeling that this current belief system is working against the natural order, as the money is not *fully* circulated within Society. Certainly, the money supplied from government bonds is circulated constantly, but the interest paid to private banks is taken out of the system and, therefore, leads to the need for more new money to meet those repayments.

> *Both Adam Smith and John Maynard Keynes, the founding fathers of our modern financial beliefs, agreed that the success of these beliefs was fundamentally dependent upon the full and constant circulation of all money.* JTC

This does not happen in Nature, where every single aspect contributes to the process of birth, growth and nourishment, as previously identified. It is here that the proponents of *public* banking have attracted my attention, as they argue that, by the government taking back the ability to print its own money, this money *and the interest it earns* could then be re-circulated back into Society.

The government would have its own printing press and the value of the money would be guaranteed from the resources managed by the government, including a country's natural resources. Here, we can see how the value of the money in circulation has a tangible value which is, once again, tied to our Planetary resources.

Returning the interest to Society would enable and support a financial system where no income tax would be necessary. Society would pay for its infrastructures of education, healthcare and social services from the interest paid on the government loans.

> *A government that owns its own bank can keep the interest and reinvest it locally, resulting in government savings of an estimated 35% to 40% just in interest. Costs can be reduced, and taxes can be cut or services can be increased. Banking and credit can become public utilities, sustaining the local economy rather than mining it for private gain; and banks can again become safe places to store our money.*
>
> SOURCE: WEB OF DEBT BY ELLEN BROWN

I am no financier, but Public banking does seem to function more in line with the Natural order. Perhaps there is a place for it in financing the social needs of Society and nurturing small businesses to grow, something that we know private banks are less interested in.

The Private banks would be there when those small businesses have become successful and take their place on the international stage, alongside the already established international and global corporations.

Public banking functions efficiently alongside private banks in countries such as Canada, India and Switzerland – the latter being no small endorsement as the heart of global banking. Indeed, 40% of the banks on this Planet are public banks, many of which are in BRIC countries; in fact, 99% of China's banks are public-owned, which is evidence of why they have weathered the recent economic chaos so well.

In America, the Bank of North Dakota came into being in 1919 and, as it fast approaches its centenary, is evidence of the positive support and nurture it has consistently made to the financial management of the State and its communities.

The following is extracted from Web of Debt by Ellen H Brown with the author's kind permission.

> ***The State Bank Option: The Bank of North Dakota***
>
> *Meanwhile, something that might get more traction because it is closer to conventional banking practice is for a state to own its own bank. The bank could then use standard fractional reserve banking principles to create credit in its books, leveraging its deposit base into loans as all banks do. Publicly-owned banks are common in India, Switzerland, Canada and other countries, where they peacefully co-exist alongside privately-owned banks.*
>
> *The colony of Pennsylvania pioneered this approach in the United States, but today only one state owns its own bank – North Dakota. The bank of North Dakota (BND) was formed in 1919 specifically to free farmers and small businessmen from the clutches of out-of-state bankers and railroad men. The BND's stated mission is to deliver sound financial services that promote agriculture, commerce and industry in North Dakota. By law, the state must deposit all its funds in the bank. The bank's earnings belong to the state, and their use is at the discretion of the state legislature. The BND is set up as a dba: 'the State of North Dakota doing business as the Bank of North Dakota.' Technically, that makes the capital of the state the capital of the bank. The BND's return on equity is about 25 per cent. It pays a hefty dividend to the state, projected at over $60 million in 2009. In the last decade, the BND has turned back a third of a billion dollars to the state's general fund, offsetting taxes. As an agent of the state, the BND can make subsidized loans to spur economic and agricultural development, and it is more lenient than other banks in pressing foreclosures. It avoids friction with private North Dakota banks by partnering with them to loan money to farmers, real estate developers, small businesses and schools. The BND maintains a robust student loan business and is one of the nation's leading banks in the number of student loans issued. It also purchases*

municipal bonds from public institutions and operates as the state's 'Mini Fed', clearing checks for more than 100 banks around the state. It is not part of the FDIC system but is self-insured by the state.

North Dakota remains fiscally sound when other state governments are swimming in red ink. By July 2009, it was one of only two states (along with Montana) able to meet their budgets. In fact, it touted the largest budget surplus it had ever had, and it had the lowest unemployment rate in the country. The state's fiscal track record is particularly impressive considering that its economy consists largely of isolated farms in an inhospitable climate. Ready, low interest credit from its own state owned bank helps explain this unusual success.

Certainly, there can be no argument that, in those areas of the globe where we practise the beliefs of private banking, Society is now being submerged by the sheer enormity of the costs of debt-supplied money. My very real concern is that the current financial crisis will continue for a long time into the future. This, I am convinced, will have serious repercussions by diverting our attention away from the far greater threat of looming food and water shortages, sparking global nuclear conflict, if our current dominant beliefs continue.

Author's Note

I am indebted to Ellen H Brown, Chairman of the Public Banking Institute in America and author of 11 books, including Web of Debt. I found this book to be an incredible and comprehensive source as to how our money supply works, its history and the role Public Banking could play in complementing our current beliefs … all accompanied with a background from the Wizard of Oz! Ellen also writes regularly on the issues of Public Banking.

Democracy – Humanity's Greatest Challenge

> *Democracy is the discipline by which we hand our personal power over to others, and then manage what they do with it. They do not take our power away from us; we give it to them willingly and with trust. When we do not manage effectively, that trust is abused. We then have to begin the discipline afresh, by taking back our power – without conflict in the case of Magna Carta or, sadly, often through conflict in the case of the French and Russian Revolutions, for example – before deciding what next to do with it.* JTC

It was in Greece that the first democracy was created (from the Greek word *demokratia – rule of the people*) back in the 5th century BC. It recognised the fact that we *all* have a contribution to make in Society, no matter how large or small.

It is the means by which we, as a species, demonstrate our level of comfort with the direction we are taking, or being directed to. Whilst the most common use of the word 'democracy' is to refer to the political process and the will of the people to command, its application can be found across all human activity.

In our personal relationships, a bonding takes place when two or more people are able to establish a common agenda and manage it through the will of each person, in an ongoing process of give and take.

In the corporate world, this translates into the popularity, or otherwise, of the goods and services provided by seller to buyer – we *vote* with our feet.

In our political and religious activity, we will once again only support the belief systems of those institutions that maintain our confidence and goodwill. Here, we will exercise our right to change by supporting, or not, the status of those institutions and their sway upon Society.

Attempts have been made throughout our history to encapsulate this process in written form. The most famous was, of course, Magna Carta. This, in turn, influenced many others charters, most recently the American Constitution.

However, history is witness to the inadequacy of these mighty works because of human fallibility. The spirit of each charter is sound in stating the rights by which we are entitled to live our lives as fully as possible whilst interacting with each other. Its enactment and management is, however, more challenging than perhaps we are prepared to admit.

If we examine this aspect a little more closely we find that, by following the will of the people, we are seeking to create a balanced Society. This balance is achieved through the diverse views and opinions of those people, reigning in any excessive use of power that is motivated by narrow beliefs of vested interest that are not beneficially supporting the majority.

It is essential therefore that we have a responsible outlet for constructive criticism of what we do, that can delve unhindered into any and all of Society's nooks and crannies to root out abuse. That, to my mind, has always been best achieved through investigative journalism provided by a *free* press. Be it in Politics, Business, Religion, individuals, or groups their record of bringing offenders of Society's values to account, has been exemplary.

The professional manner in which the classified information provided by someone like Edward Snowden for example, was sifted and vetted before being put in the public domain, ensured that only knowledge about potential abuse was available for public debate and, as time passes by, national security does not appear to have been threatened, as far as we are aware to date. In this particular case the outcry across the planet at international surveillance measures of the magnitude these disclosures revealed, and introduced without public debate, highlights how critical the work of the media is now becoming.

In this age of digital information, where anyone can publish *unverified data and be damned,* it is critical that the necessary resource, with responsible checks and balances, is permanently in place to draw Society's attention to human fallibility.

That can only come from a free press that is itself carefully overseen and licensed to do its work. In this manner Society can draw confidence that it has at last created a means with which to effectively and responsibly manage its journey along the evolutionary path.

And when misuse of resources occurs, as was the case with the phone hacking scandal in the UK, there must also be draconian penalties, not merely financial, with imprisonment and public disgrace of all involved, be they acting in a professional capacity or not.

In this new global era the integrity of the data that can now be put into the public domain has to be established at all costs, to maintain the respect of not only those being investigated but also those being protected. This, to my mind, has to be the core responsibility of a free press. There is no other alternative for a Society seeking a healthy, vibrant and balanced Democracy.

Democracy today

Modern democracy has become dominated by political *parties* who demand total allegiance to the party view and doctrines. By ushering the vast majority of the people we elect to office under *party umbrellas*, control of the power wielded by government can be managed more effectively by the party elite.

Democracy, therefore, becomes increasingly the will of the *party* that dominates rather than the will of the people. *Candidates are selected by the party and offered to the people.* Manifestos promoted at election time are often worded in such a way as to allow wide interpretation of what they are actually promising and what can happen.

With the ever-growing costs involved in getting elected, it becomes essential for a party to be as attractive as possible to corporate sponsors who are capable of this level of finance.

The attraction to business is, of course, the ability to improve the chances of meeting its own goals by influencing government decision-making. A *party*-controlled government can offer reassurance to business that it is capable of delivering on promises made in return for corporate support, in whatever shape this takes.

This becomes a double-edged sword for those we entrust with managing the political process. On the one hand, democratically elected representatives are tasked with the duties of serving the people, by managing the taxpayer funds and meeting the needs of Society.

> *It was Machiavelli and Aristotle who expressed the view that the judgements of the majority may well be flawed, but are nonetheless more trustworthy than the commands of the elite. It is a natural phenomenon that the credentials and/or honours of these elite are incapable of matching the collective intelligence of the majority.* JTC

At the same time, however, as fallible human beings they can also find themselves serving a vested interest that has *financed* them rather than *elected* them. Whether it is the wishes of the voter, or its sponsors, that control the direction of important issues such as climate change, it becomes a challenge of monumental proportions for any government.

This conflict of interest can only ever result in a loss of trust by one side or the other. The year 2008 saw the deepening of a rift between the elected and electors with the use of public money to bail out private banking. At the heart of this perceived abuse was the misuse of public funds, further aggravated by the fact that no authorisation had been sought from the people, whose money it was in the first place.

There is another symptom of the current weak democratic process in the guise of the European Union and its proliferation of Eurozone projects, which are unsupported by any mechanism for popular democratic mandate.

Within an environment that lacks democratic checks and balances, money and power has become master. Tax revenues are spent without proper accountability, evidenced by the Union's formal accounts not having been given a clean bill of health for 19 *consecutive* years, because of *irregularities.*

It would also appear from the auditor's report on the 2011 budget, controls on 86% of the organisation's spending were deemed to be only partially effective.

Whilst I accept that the amount of money involved is vast, this very fact would dictate that, after so many years without proper resolve, something, somewhere, is fundamentally flawed. Whether it is a flawed process of money management, or a total lack of respect for money taken from the wages of working people, again challenges the probity of the current system as I have previously mentioned.

Abuse of the democratic process in this fashion creates a political *power bubble* in which the goals and ambitions of vested interest, both inside and outside of the *party,* flourish at the expense of elector needs.

Indeed, social needs for anything, from pensions to health care and employment, are currently being critically reduced to repay sovereign debt. This, in turn, has seen many public services sold off to business, resulting in higher costs to the consumer and reduced services. At the same time, there is a greater deregulation of corporate activity in order, we are told, to support the international business community in the creation of jobs.

A New 'Unelected' Democracy

The power shift that has occurred, in which the actions of elected representatives are increasingly governed by the criteria of *unelected* corporations and financial markets, is now eroding faith in the fundamental democratic process that has previously existed between electors and elected, evidenced in dwindling voter turnout at election time.

This situation is further exacerbated as unelected ratings agencies like Moody's and Standard & Poor's are increasingly holding sway over the democratic process, applying their own narrow financial criteria in assessing a country's viability and Society's standards.

The careers of politicians are increasingly measured, not by the broad spectrum of the contribution they make to the welfare of the Society that elected them, but to the narrow confine of their ability to manage, or not, the repayment of national debt and the maintenance of their country's credit rating.

This was evidenced in Greece in 2011, when the financial plight of the country saw the then Prime Minister decide to hold a referendum with the Greek people on a suitable course of action, as it would be them shouldering the repayment of debt for their lifetimes and beyond.

> *They didn't take India away from us. We gave it to them.*
>
> PARAPHRASED FROM MAHATMA GANDHI

Immediately, other political leaders, and the financial markets, went into a state of apoplexy at the very notion of involving the electorate, placing so much pressure upon the Greek Prime Minister that he reversed his decision and lost his job.

This was followed up both in Greece and Italy by a further erosion of the democratic process as *unelected* Technocrats were brought in to run government. Their task is driven within a very narrow perspective that primarily seeks to ensure and maintain the country's ability to repay its debts.

Unelected, and with a remit far removed from the traditional functions of elected government, there is now a priority on reducing the costs of supplying the traditional services that support Society, as well as selling off public utilities (including water) to repay debt, which the people have no say over.

In 2012, the International Monetary Fund, European Central Bank and European Union demanded written guarantees from all the elected parties in Greece that the austerity measures will be continued *regardless of any future elections.*

(How this is enforced, if a future government takes office that comprises none of the parties or elected representatives who signed the original undertaking, is a situation that only time will answer.)

Here, we get to the very heart of the challenges now facing us, and why democracy is vital to our proper functioning as a species with its essential checks and balances on how we interact. Current dominant financial thinking is stifling the true democratic process, creating an imbalance where money is now both *'The Master' of those who have it and those who don't!*

> *Whilst the core essence of our power resides in our ability to create and experience Life, of equal importance is our ability to effectively manage the environment we create. That is the purpose of Democracy.* JTC

The Challenge in a nutshell

This continuing erosion of democracy is effectively returning our species to the slavery of the 13th century, and global slavery at that. It is best identified in the phrase a *lost generation*, describing the ever frightening numbers of young unemployed who have little prospect, in the current climate, of fulfilling their most basic Life purpose – to create, support and nurture a home and family of their own.

This is yet another of the colossal problems we now confront in a cataclysmic situation, where dominant financial beliefs are actually going head to head with the omnipotent forces of Nature, because of a weakened democratic process.

In trying to manage Life purely by financial values and disciplines, we are increasingly impeding our ability to follow the human life cycles that are an intrinsic part of who and what we are as a species.

A belief that the minority can sustain Life on Earth through the domination of their beliefs and views is a myth. Life can only be sustained through the huge diversity of all things integral to this Planet.

That is why no single belief system has ever achieved total domination in our entire history. The majority hold the consensus as to the balance of Life here. It is the birthplace of all dissention, new leadership and new beliefs … it always has been and it always will be.

We operate in a rhythm and flow of stimuli that repeats itself with monotonous regularity. The assault on democracy in the West is no different to what happened in Rome and resulted in the fall of the Empire. Power created abuse, which created distrust, which led to collapse. We need to better manage our fallibilities.

Fighting against this natural order has always been the breeding ground for serious conflict, as these omnipotent forces begin to react against any man-made restricting beliefs that impede our progress.

The conflict will arise as the supporters of our current beliefs try desperately to hold on to the status quo, fervently resisting its gradual dismantling as Evolution returns us to a more natural and balanced environment, governed by a broader spectrum of beliefs.

I say this because I believe that democracy is an intrinsic part of our make-up as a species. Both sides are fully aware when abuse takes place and eventually it reaches a tipping point, where the arrogance inherent within the abuse being perpetrated can no longer be tolerated by the majority.

There is evidence of this intolerance now appearing across the broad Western political arena as we hear outcries from our media of increasing intervention by governments in what and how they report, along with an increasing surveillance of Society. This form of totalitarianism is not only unhealthy and dangerous but reflects a growing public unrest in lower turnouts at election time and also reducing membership numbers of the traditional political parties.

'In the early 1950s three million Britons were paid-up Conservatives and the number remained over one million for much of the 1980s. When David Cameron became leader in 2005, membership stood at 258,000 and has fallen steadily since.' Current estimates believe it to be around the 100,000 level (Source: *The Independent*).

> *Change is the one constant in Life ... either we manage it, or it will manage us.*
> JTC

The very essence of democracy is that it is the tool by which we, as a species, bring balance to Life. This balance cannot be written in a book of rules, as it is something we sense deep within us, providing the ability to collectively know when imbalance occurs. Only physical force can maintain that imbalance, as we see in developing countries like Zimbabwe, but it cannot be maintained forever and eventually the abusers fall. In the more *joined up* world of the internet and globalisation I believe these corrections will begin to happen much more quickly.

I now find myself once again repeating my mantra, that none of what is written here is a judgement. There are no *good* or *bad* people in all of this. Rather, it offers a perfect example of how we function as a species. We are constantly developing new ways and means by which to experience Life, and how well or badly we manage what we create is reflected in the healthiness, or otherwise, of a truly democratic process.

By accepting that we are a diverse species, interacting in a diverse world, we can see that no *single* belief system – be it financial, corporate, religious or political – can be made to work satisfactorily for our long-term support or benefit. It is incapable of satisfying the plethora of needs demanded by our natural diversity.

The present democratic process has changed little since Ancient Greece, hence Aristotle's observations given earlier. The challenge we now face as a species is for a complete overhaul of how we manage Society and *on what terms the 99% hand over their power*, recognising just how much we have evolved as a species since those days.

The Internet – Humanity's Mirror

As we evolve into the new Technological Age, the Internet is having the single greatest impact upon our species and how we live Life. It is rapidly becoming the global artery of humankind, as its veins filter off (eventually) to every member of our species. It is certainly introducing a new kind of democracy as our uncensored thoughts, beliefs, ideas and creations flow out and rebound to every corner of the Planet.

Because of this, there is absolutely no doubt in my mind that the Internet is *Evolutionary*, and not *Revolutionary*. Aggression is not a function of Evolution, but rather a symptom, illustrated throughout our history by the efforts of the old to quash the birth of the new in a hopeless endeavour to preserve the status quo.

The overwhelming argument for me that the Internet is *Evolutionary* can be seen in this powerful tool's ability to not only provide us with a truly democratic capability, but also, and even more interesting, a gigantic *mirror*, into which we can look to find out more about how we function as a species – warts and all!

> *He who knows others is wise. He who knows himself is enlightened.*
>
> LAO TZU

In the early years, I saw statistics that showed over 60% of web content was pornographic. Our obsession with sex has been documented since early cave drawings and is not limited to any particular sector of Society.

Whilst we are repulsed by aggressive images of abuse to women and children, it demonstrates how the new technology we have created presents us with an uncensored picture of who and what we are all about through this totally non-judgemental mirror.

Our obsession with pornography is a difficult pill to swallow and many valiant attempts are continually made to rid Society of its more extreme activity. However, what the Web is effectively demonstrating to us is that sex, and our different attitudes to it, is a powerful force in human behaviour, and that it is now becoming increasingly difficult to brush under Society's vast carpet.

As with all Evolutionary developments, huge controversy surrounds its use and application. Its potential for surveillance and the impact this could have upon our basic rights to live our lives in total freedom, whilst respecting and adhering to the laws of the land, is now becoming Society's greatest concern.

Perhaps there is justification for this concern as any decisions resulting from data-driven analysis, and particularly that of how humanity is living Life, can only ever be partially correct. If *all* interpretations of data only ever offer the perspective of the people who interpret that data, **and each person's interpretation will be different and limited to their own personal biases,** then we run considerable risk of serious abuses of the majority.

In the case of terrorism, this risk has already resulted in a substantial reduction in the traditional freedoms of the majority and our enjoyment of Life. The extreme views and activity of all beliefs, be they religious, political or corporate have disrupted Society, and will continue to, in varying degrees, as history is witness to, no matter how draconian the measures we invoke to resist them (and this includes pornography).

This, to my mind, begs the question as to whether it would be prudent to actually ask Society how much protection it wants and at what cost to its personal freedom. Governments are currently in a difficult situation by trying to impose levels of oversight and transparency upon Society that they seem reticent to impose upon their own activities.

Any debate this last point introduces must have positive repercussions, in helping us to more clearly define and draw the line in the use and impact our growing data-based technology has upon our Evolution as a species. This must become a priority in the duty we all owe to each other because of the impact it will have upon how we shape our future – a totalitarian state, or true democracy.

2012 – The Internet ... an Ending and a Beginning

Whilst we have only looked at how this mirror can cause repression, there are many positive *reflections* it casts in how we function democratically. There are few who would argue that the Internet offers the perfect vehicle for us to provide supportive action in times of natural disaster anywhere in the world, at a speed never before experienced.

It supports our commercial and social desires across eBay, Facebook, YouTube, 38 Degrees, Avaaz etc., and many other platforms, reflecting characteristics that are *common to all of us* and not the province of any one race, colour, gender or creed.

Any mirror will reflect every aspect presented to it and the Internet identifies and recognises how quickly we now form our own groups and communities of like-minded people. It allows us to see more clearly the vast myriad of interests we have, as a single species, that stimulate us to interact individually and collectively on a daily basis.

Increasingly, in these austere times, these groups come into being because our traditional institutions are failing us, making them less effective in supporting our needs as individuals and communities. Here, we see a true reflection of our evolving Society, as this impotence is countered by an explosion of self-help groups.

These growing social networks are further evidence of the hand of Evolution at work because of the entirely *organic* growth in use of this phenomenon that is the World Wide Web. I am sure its founder, Sir Tim Berners-Lee, would agree that his brainchild has already exceeded his early expectations in how it is influencing and supporting change in every facet of our lives.

Instead of the traditional *top down* direction of our activity by committees and autocrats, it is providing simple infrastructures that make it possible for *all* of us to determine our own lateral interaction and direction with each other.

Here we are at our most comfortable as we present and act out our own personal creations in an unfettered environment. It is also here that I see the hand of 2012 most vividly; in the *ending* of the old, restricting ways of interacting as the Evolutionary process *begins* the new through this technology.

Any beliefs that traditionally *separated* us will no longer carry credibility in the face of new *uniting* beliefs and actions caused by the non-judgemental mirror effect of this evolving technology that is now spurring our globalisation.

> *Who would have thought, even a year ago, that Egyptians would march on their US Embassy demanding fair treatment for Americans because of Occupy Oakland?*
>
> JTC, OCTOBER 2011

This new world already has its own markets and communications systems, and it will not be long before it has its own established banking and political systems that better democratise money and how we manage our affairs.

F A Hayek, in his book, *Denationalisation of Money,* describes how money is just a commodity like grain, petrol or steel. By creating a truly independent banking system, inflation could become a thing of the past as private companies, with their own currencies, compete against each other for our business.

In similar fashion, as mentioned earlier, we are now seeing the birth of virtual currencies as the Internet itself breeds its own money supply through sites such as Bitcoin, Litecoin and OpenCoin.

The Internet and People Power

In the political arena, a new and potent democratic process is emerging from the increasing use of the Internet, with more and more direction coming from the people.

They are devising their own petitions and agendas, which political leadership are increasingly heeding and acting upon. This is evidenced by the work of Avaaz globally, 38 Degrees in the UK, MoveOn in the United States, GetUp in Australia and a whole new breed of lobbying organisations.

By 2013, the number of people supporting Avaaz, for example, has increased to over 25 million ... and growing.

Working together with a similar UK-based group, 38 Degrees.org.uk, we witnessed the true impact of this new *web democracy*. Here, one of the world's most powerful men, Rupert Murdoch, was stopped from expanding his interests in fully acquiring the broadcaster BskyB – something that had been seen as a forgone conclusion in political circles before this intervention.

This, and the multitude of other campaigns, is demonstrating our growing unification as a species and is never more in evidence than when using the services of organisations such as Avaaz. As soon as you enter their site, displayed on the screen is a rolling list of the names and countries of people across the globe supporting the latest petition.

You become immediately aware that your decision to act is being supported by other like-minded people around the world, irrespective of the traditional *uniforms* of race, colour, creed, or gender – *and without even speaking to them.*

> *A massive online campaign by the Avaaz community in Brazil has just won a stunning victory against corruption.*
>
> *The 'clean record' law was a bold proposal that banned any politician convicted of crimes like corruption and money laundering from running for office. With nearly 25% of the Congress under investigation for corruption, most said it would never pass. But after Avaaz launched the largest online campaign in Brazilian history, helping to build a petition of over 2 million signatures, 500,000 online actions, and tens of thousands of phone calls, we won!*
>
> *Avaaz members fought corrupt congressmen daily as they tried every trick in the book to kill, delay, amend, and weaken the bill, and won the day every time. The bill passed Congress, and already over 330 candidates for office face disqualification!*
>
> *One Brazilian member wrote to us when the law was passed, saying:*
>
> *'I have never been as proud of the Brazilian people as I am today! Congratulations to all that have signed. Today, I feel like an actual citizen with political power.' – Silvia.*
>
> *Our strategy in Brazil was simple: make a solution so popular and visible that it can't be opposed, and be so vigilant that we can't be ignored.*

This victory shows what our community can do – at a national level, in developing nations, and on the awful problem of corruption. Anywhere in the world, we can build legislative proposals to clean up corruption in government, back them up with massive citizen support, and fight legislators who try to block them.

France's Le Monde called our 'impressive and unprecedented petition' campaign a 'spectacular political and moral victory for civil society.' And, while this victory may be a first, we can make it the precedent for global citizen action.

Amazingly, our entire Brazil campaign was made possible by just a couple of Avaaz team members, serving over 600,000 Avaaz members in Brazil. The power of the Avaaz model is that technology can enable a tiny team to help millions of people work together on the most pressing issues. It's one of the most powerful ways a small donation can make a difference in the world.

Some 5.6 million of us are reading this email — if a small fraction of us donate just $3 or $5 per week, or 50 cents per day, the entire Avaaz team will be funded and we can even expand our work on corruption and a range of issues. Click below to become a Sustainer of Avaaz and help take our anti-corruption campaigning global:

https://secure.avaaz.org/en/donate/

We've seen the heart-wrenching movies about street kids and desperate urban poverty in Brazil, and we know that, across the world, political corruption preys on our communities and saps human potential. In Brazil, our community has helped turn the tide and usher in a new era of transparent, accountable politics. Let's seize the opportunity and begin to fight corruption everywhere it's needed today.

With hope, Rick, Luis, Graziela, David, Ben, Maria Paz, Benjamin and the entire Avaaz Team. July 2010

REPRINTED WITH THEIR KIND PERMISSION

The Internet has moved democracy to new levels of global understanding and application – something not even considered in our wildest dreams just 25 years ago.

In spite of just 39% of the global population using the Web in 2013 (Source: Wikipedia), its impact upon our way of life is without precedent. JTC

Its impact has vertically expanded the traditional democratic model, by enabling people to express their views and opinions to their institutions and each other *directly*. It has also expanded horizontally by transcending out-of-date beliefs, providing true equality of access to women and young people who might previously have been excluded.

The speed with which we have formed social groups, which transcend all previous boundaries, is probably the single most influential factor in merging us into a Global Village. It is also a true reflection of *village* life that trends, injustices and gossip now fly across the globe in milliseconds, as we share our experiences of Life with each other.

Unlike conventional villages, however, we do not know those we share information with as *physical* neighbours, work colleagues, or through the intimacy of a shared physical location. This anonymity is probably one of the most influential factors in breaking down the traditionally judgemental barriers that have previously separated us, bringing us together now as who and what we really are … a single species.

Sitting in front of screens, we are becoming members of *like-minded groups*, rather than residents of demographic areas. We quickly find and share our personal interests through the collective enthusiasm of people situated in diverse countries and continents around the Planet.

I see the Internet as a global *stage* which anyone may approach and mount. Here, we can present ourselves, unhindered, to our fellow men and women in whatever guise we choose – speaker, trader, writer, musician/artist – and they can reflect back their reactions to our presence in front of them, similarly unhindered.

There is no doubt in my mind that we are now seeing the materialisation of what has previously been referred to as the *collective consciousness*, as we share and recognise our thoughts, fears, ambitions and values directly with each other.

The impact of this powerful tool has not even begun to demonstrate how it will shape the Society of the future – but shape it it certainly will and in the most democratic of fashions, as we accept and adapt to our new environment.

> *In 'gifting' the Web to humanity without personal reward, has Sir Tim Berners-Lee influenced the strong desire by users to keep this powerful facility pure of intent?* JTC

Although it is still early days, what is also evident is the difficulty our traditional institutions are having in trying to influence how we use the Internet. Corporate efforts to gain acceptance within this medium, other than as an adjunct to their existing business, seem to fall short no matter how their methods change.

Even the mighty Facebook has experienced negative reaction from its millions of users when allowing advertisers access to members. Indeed, its problems around the time of its flotation on the stock market were centred upon this very aspect. And this happens time and time again as site owners endeavour to better capitalise upon their regular audiences.

Certainly, there are times when we are amenable to advertising, but it is a wary process by site owners, who juggle an income from their audience with watching closely any adverse reaction which might see that audience quickly moving away.

Maybe this is another example of the new emergent collective *unconscious* at work, as we react against the relentless invasion of our privacy by telesales, direct mail and doorstep canvassing, ever present in the traditional areas of our lives.

Here, we can actually experience a purer type of democracy, something that is disappearing outside of the Web, where spin and political subservience to corporate need have bred a feeling of impotence in Society at large.

This is the basic structure of how eBay, Amazon, Facebook, Twitter and all other sites function. They provide *platforms* upon this global stage, where we can interact with each other, without interference, coercion or pressure from vested interest.

Within these infrastructures we see an incorruptible democracy in action as we give our unbiased assessment of another's activity, be it trading on eBay or offering a point of view on Twitter or Facebook. Provided we do not overstep the rules of common courtesy and respect, our assessment can be as pointed as we choose.

I believe this truly transparent democracy aligns closely with who and what we are, and meets our deep and constant desire for integrity in our dealings with each other. Interestingly, I also believe that, as we increasingly take this growing transparency for granted, it highlights ever brighter the lack of accountability and transparency from our traditional institutions as whistle-blower activity continues unabated.

It begs the question as to whether there will come a time when we demand the protocols of the Internet across the whole arena of human interaction, personally, institutionally, locally and globally.

The Internet – People Politics Instead of Party Politics

In the political arena, its impact has powerfully changed the traditional methods we have used. The election of Barack Obama in 2008 not only broke new ground in American politics, but shook the very foundations of the then electoral process.

Here, corporate America had previously exercised a large say in the election process, but the Internet drove a coach and horses through this controlled environment.

Whilst his opponents sought the vast amounts of money necessary to mount a political campaign from the only sector previously capable of providing this largesse, namely the corporate sector, President Obama received huge support from individual electors and the like through the medium of the Internet, in addition to the corporate sector.

So profound was the impact of this development on the then status quo that, within months of his election, the US Judiciary overturned a 20-year law put in place to limit the amount of financial support corporations were able to give to candidates.

The independence of the Judiciary is not the province of this book. However, their actions through *Citizens United* are evidence of the impact the new era of the Internet is having upon the traditional way of doing things. The power this young medium has already shown cannot be ignored in its capability to meet a vital aspect of our need as a species for a truly Democratic process.

This is particularly pertinent at a time when solutions are being sought to the growing apathy demonstrated by electors towards the election process, particularly in the West.

The use of the Internet was seen as a possible solution to the problem, but this has its flaws. The risks of this sensitive electronic data being hacked and abused, no matter how small, is seen as something that we can ill afford with such a critical aspect of democratic decision-making.

To my mind, we attain the very best and most accurate assessment of political popularity and support when people physically turn out to elect their chosen representative, this effort reinforcing our need to strive and achieve.

Our physical appearance at polling booths shows a strong involvement and commitment to a system that represents the very pulse of a healthy Society. It seems to me to be an essential part of the current process – until we create something else.

Another contributor to voter apathy is the seeming impotence of the individual when confronted by the almost limitless financial support that is offered to candidates by the corporate sector, as they seek to further their vested interest. There has been talk of limiting corporate sponsorship, but this can be difficult to police.

Alternatively, it has been suggested that there should be no corporate sponsorship and that the parties should be funded out of the public purse. Again, it could be argued that this can restrict the democratic process by placing limits upon who might stand. A plethora of independent candidates could prove expensive, and with a much lower overall chance of being elected.

The experience with Barack Obama might point the way ahead, by returning to the purest of democratic processes possible through the use of the Internet. Here, its ability to provide a *platform* offers the perfect means by which we might elect and entrust people with the power to manage the requirements of an ever-changing Society.

To attract public purse sponsorship, anyone with something to say could stand up and see how many like-minded people she or he might attract by their views.

The strength of this attraction would be further demonstrated by the level of both financial support and votes those like-minded people then provided to help the candidate into office.

Once a nominated target figure for both is achieved, then the candidate would become eligible for public support. This type of approach would also reintroduce greater democracy to the people, as anyone could stand without seeking or requiring the acceptance of an established political party.

This last point is not to be underestimated in importance in reducing current voter apathy, and stimulating a greater sense of voter responsibility, from a newly-inspired sense of involvement in how their lives are run. *People* politics instead of Party politics!

With an elected representative supported by the voters it would also become difficult, if not impossible, to avoid direct accountability to voters whose money they had taken, strengthening the relationship between electors and elected.

Already, crowdfunding sites such as Kickstarter and Indiegogo have become very popular in backing anything from entertainment to construction. Someone with a project opens it up to public scrutiny and, if appealing, financial support is forthcoming from that public.

Whilst established crowdfunding activity has an emphasis upon business projects, this can be easily expanded into the political arena. This is evidenced by its application for raising money to provide a stenographer in the trial of Bradley (now Chelsea) Manning. Although successful, the court subsequently denied access to this facility, a subject that is outside the province of this book.

Crowdfunding does demonstrate just how powerful a tool it has the potential to become, in bringing greater balance back to the democratic process by empowering people to act and be heard, creating a true *People's Parliament.*

Certainly there is evidence of how the Internet is injecting fresh enthusiasm back into politics as the activities of organisations such as 38 Degrees, provide people with a new and growing sense of empowerment.

Whilst this is only a thumbnail sketch, the Internet has been tested for its contribution to the Democratic process and not found wanting, and it will be interesting to see how and what we create to take this whole process further.

The Real power behind the Internet

Finally, and of critical significance to our personal development, is our newfound ability to decide how we want to co-exist with our neighbours in our growing Global Village. This is based upon the Internet's unfailing ability to provide *unedited* thoughts, activities and visions about how we see our World and reflect them across the Planet.

Included in this are the reactions of the 99% to the 1% and vice versa. Traditional abuses on both sides are immediately placed in the spotlight, from cyber-attacks to any forms of repression. This is not something that has been designed into the system, but happens because by its very nature it faithfully records and projects our thoughts and actions upon the global stage.

In such an open environment, the foundations are being set for us to create a whole new world that is built upon our learning from the mistakes of the past. Indeed, it is becoming difficult, if not impossible, to recreate the mistakes and abuses of the past in such an open and transparent environment, something it will take time for us to accept and become comfortable with.

We have the abilities to create a new world if we want to – it is what we have always excelled at – and now we have created the technology to support that task. We simply need to support leaders who do not feel threatened by this new environment, but who will *serve and unite* by recognising and encouraging a truly transparent and accountable Society, driven by a Democratic belief system that will support our future survival.

> *When we go to the people*
>
> *Live among the people*
>
> *Learn from them*
>
> *Start with what they know*
>
> *Build on what they have.*
>
> *But of the best leaders*
>
> *When their task is accomplished*
>
> *Their work is done*
>
> *The people will say ...*
>
> *WE HAVE DONE IT OURSELVES.*

OLD CHINESE PROVERB

A New Democratic Environment for the 21st Century

The previous chapter has illustrated how the necessary levels of transparency and accountability needed to return trust to Society might be achieved in a manner never before possible, because of the Internet.

For this foundation block to shoulder its burden effectively, we also have to accept our collective involvement and responsibility in creating a new and truly Democratic process. No longer can the traditional apathy of the electorate continue, as we have now learnt to our cost.

> *The flaw in how we perceive Democracy occurs when we give our power away, allow others to take control, and give up on our responsibility to ensure the process remains accountable. The Internet is now providing the opportunity for change.* JTC

Fundamental to this process is the need to accept how creative and fallible we are, and that we will always need effective checks and balances to guard against the human fallibility that has repeatedly pulled us down in the past.

And, at the moment of this acceptance, along with a determination to confront and better manage our fallibilities, we lift our game as a species to higher levels of integrity and achievement than have ever been possible before.

Electing leadership who recognise and support this simple but powerful change in our thinking will, I believe, introduce a new sense of human purpose across the broad spectrum of our growing Global Society.

With an increasing acceptance of accountability and transparency at all strata of Society, where do we begin the construction of our new Democratic model? What shape will it take, and how will it function to minimise a return to the abuses of the past?

> *We cannot contemplate confronting or managing the current challenges to Society without a new and significant contribution from that Society.* JTC

As a species of Creators, we demand the discipline of integrity for the sole purpose of evaluating whether our creations work or do not work for our collective benefit.

The critical importance of integrity, to us as a species, is evidenced by the growth of activity in the first decade of this 21st century from *whistle-blowers* delivering previously suppressed material into the public arena.

If we are able to look more deeply into this activity, *without resorting to judgement and blame*, we can see how the mistakes, or vested interest of those in power, which had previously been suppressed or distorted by spin, has eventually been brought into the public domain for scrutiny.

A whistle-blower is not specially trained or educated for what they do. It is something deep within every one of us that recognises when the agenda of vested interest is acting against the best interests of the majority. It is then, out of a deep sense of balance, that we are driven to bring these agendas to the attention of the many.

> *There is a line over which we do not tread – it is a part of the collective consciousness. We instinctively know when something is unacceptable to our common good. It is demonstrated by the growing number of 'whistle-blowers' within closed institutional buildings – no matter what area of Life they are acting within.* JTC

To manage this aspect of the human condition in a more beneficial manner, rather than the clandestine environment necessary for whistle-blowers to function at present, we must create an authentic and democratically respected means by which checks and balances are able to operate, and complements the workings of a truly free and accountable press.

A New Tier to Democracy

> *Magna Carta came into force on 15th June 1215. Of particular significance was a section now called clause 61, which established a committee of 25 nobles who oversaw what the king was up to. They had powers to overrule his will and even confiscate his property if he defied the dictates of the Charter.* JTC

Public Office demands that those who dedicate themselves to Society work long hours and travel great distances in discharging their duties. It is up to Society, therefore, to demonstrate greater commitment and better support towards them in discharging those duties than has been the case in the past.

If integrity is the mortar that holds Society together, then at its centre is the judicial system I have alluded to earlier. This tried and tested service offers a respectable template for the formation of a second tier of scrutiny across Society. In place of juries, there would be public panels with access to what we create and manage for our collective use.

Their primary purpose would be to provide a porthole through which we are able to view all of our institutional infrastructures, providing hands-on observations, checks and balances that were previously carried out by trade watchdogs.

It cannot be stressed enough that judgement is not the purpose of this type of oversight but, like any accomplished manager, a commitment and concentration on the need to recognise when problems occur and support the appropriate remedy.

If we follow the judicial system, these panels would operate across as many areas of human activity as we choose. As with our courtroom jury, any citizen would be eligible to serve for a limited period on *Public Observance Panels (POPs).* Membership selection might be weighted towards people with a vested interest in a particular area.

Investors might scrutinise the workings of regulatory financial bodies – car owners, the safety standards regulators; shoppers, the food standards regulators; voters, the political regulators; patients, the health service, and so on. Society would become better informed about how it is managed and served, as well as a real involvement in those processes.

POPs would have access to non-aligned think tanks for unbiased information, advice and guidance upon the subjects they were overseeing, similar to the function provided by a judge to the jury.

As an example, the financial POP here in the UK might have access to the Institute for Fiscal Studies (IFS), providing an unbiased picture of our financial wellbeing – or otherwise.

(This respected independent think-tank accused all the main parties of failing to come clean over the depth of the cuts needed after the 2010 general election, whilst the campaigning was in full swing in the UK. I am unaware that any party responded to this call, in spite of it being a crucial factor in how the next government would shape Society during its term of office. This example, perhaps, validates the need for the type of unbiased advice POPs should receive.)

The introduction of this *POP culture* would go a long way to spreading responsibility across Society for how we manage what we create – bringing back into Society the greater levels of trust and support we now so desperately need, through a healthier, non-judgemental, open and active democracy.

> *With the necessary checks and balances, POP members would be able to report on Facebook and the like as to the activities of the committee with the minutes freely available online.* JTC

For the first time in our history, POPs would actually expand the application of vested interest *to the consumer*, reintroducing balance and transparency back into Society since the bank bailouts of 2007/8.

(If the taxpayer/consumer has now become the lender of last resort for those institutions designated as 'too big to fail', it is not unreasonable that this lender is capable of overseeing and protecting its interests, in the same manner as any other institution.)

Time and again our human fallibility has been evidenced by regulatory bodies that have both vested interest and too little power over what they are regulating. This has repeatedly led to the abuse of those on the receiving end of goods and services.

Even with the greater level of transparency POPs could offer, things will, of course, still go wrong. However, in an environment where we *all* share the responsibility for what we create, we may bitch when mistakes occur, but there would be an underlying sense of fairness and balance because of the *collective* responsibility inherent in the process.

Evolution is at the Heart of this Change

We owe it to ourselves to create and maintain a healthy global democratic process across all areas of Life.

For my part, I believe this process is already underway as we see protests in one country supported by people in other countries. Who would have thought, even a year previously, that Egyptians would march on their US Embassy in 2011, demanding fair treatment for Americans because of police brutality against protestors supporting Occupy Oakland?

Dramatic changes like this illustrate the Evolutionary manner in which Democracy is changing in this 21st century and the knock-on effect this must have on the global political arena.

For this to evolve smoothly, we need to learn from our beleaguered Religious institutions and ensure our political systems evolve in line with our personal development, or suffer serious credibility problems.

Cracks are already beginning to appear as our global leaders struggle to come up with a strategy to address the growing problems of debt, diminishing global resources and climate change.

At the heart of this inability to progress lies the wisdom of Albert Einstein, which I again repeat:

> *'The thinking that created the problem is quite incapable of solving it.'*

The vested interest driving political parties will have to be recognised and current thinking adapted to find solutions that work. The increasing protests across the Planet are coming from Global Villagers who share the same concerns about the problems we are all facing.

Because these are common problems they have a *uniting* influence, which will contribute towards the birthing of a new Democracy that is underwritten by global consensus and not vested interest.

I cannot see this unity coming about through Political parties creating global headquarters, supported by a top down bureaucracy. Its very size would make it impossible to align closely with villagers. Also, its similarities to what we already have would make it difficult to change thinking and old habits in how we address our current problems.

The organic growth of loose-knit organisations, however, bonded by a common understanding and acceptance of the need for new dominating beliefs that have the support of villagers, offers the opportunity to address our problems from a new direction that reflects a global consensus:

A Democracy driven by Charitable endeavour rather than a Democracy driven by Profitable endeavour.

Freedom is the right to live as we wish.

EPICTETUS

We can never suppress our creative genius, nor should we. However, for it to continue to flourish, the Evolutionary process will demand that we create new dominant beliefs, as suggested here. Whatever the outcome, it is evident that we now need to better safeguard our quality of Life, ensuring that both our ingenuity and apathy never again threaten our immediate or long-term relationship with each other and this beautiful Planet.

Education

Our technological innovation means children are now spending nearly as much time in front of 'a screen' as they spend sleeping. Business has taken this opportunity to promote products, images, values and identities that collectively are converting young people into consumers, by shaping both their identities and their desires.

In this 21st century, the chances of a career for many of them are remote. Some went into the armed forces, putting their lives on the line in what many have called an illegal war they had no say in, only to return and join the remainder of their generation in assuming responsibility for a lifetime of debt they had no hand in creating.

Surely we owe our children something more than that provided by current traditional thinking that immerses them in huge amounts of debt, with little opportunity to repay it, thereby sowing the seeds of future rebellion within Society. Indeed, as I write, both the UK and US governments are deliberating on plans to increase the interest rates on student debt to make it easier to package and sell to earn them income. The public outcry this has unleashed is understandable, as there will be many students who will not repay this debt in their lifetime if it is handed to the private sector. If Society is supportive of this, then there are many who, I am sure, would declare that Society to be morally bankrupt. What we owe them is a new educational system that will nurture, prepare and support them to enter and eventually shape our new Global Village, as well as the all-important, on-going relationship with each other and our Planet. JTC

The urge for each one of us to find our own personal identity manifests from the moment we are born, becoming ever stronger as we reach adulthood and finally driving us to go out into the world.

During the process, we constantly question what it is that inspires and fulfils us, whether it be raising a family or growing a business; looking after animals or through artistic endeavour; nurturing the Planet or supporting its people.

This drive to find what inspires today's young is made more difficult by a rapidly changing environment. It is equally new to their parents as, collectively, we struggle with the impact of globalisation, multiculturalism and an expanding technology that is a communications *explosion*.

The Foundation of every state is the education of its youth.

DIOGENES LAERTIUS, C. AD 222–250

Never before has there been such a wide-ranging personal adjustment demanded of our Society, or of such magnitude. As I constantly repeat throughout this book, only by recognising who and what we are as a species, and applying this knowledge to better manage the way in which we interact with each other and this Planet, do we stand any chance of managing the vast social upheaval we are now experiencing.

If you accept this premise, the role of our young and their education become paramount to our future success in dealing with the many facets of these challenging times ... and we have a long road to travel. For too long we have used and abused our children, from enslavement in servitude to enslavement by debt; a sure sign of a Society with a deep moral problem.

> ***Haiti***
>
> *In a country which overthrew slavery in 1804, today it is estimated that 225,000 children live in forced servitude. They work from before sun up to after sundown, are often sexually and physically abused and usually go underfed and uneducated. UNICEF Mid-Year Review of 2010*
>
> HUMANITARIAN ACTION REPORT

Indeed, it has been widely reported in the press this year (2013) that the level of student debt in America is more than the total sum of credit card debt in the country!

The pressures on the present education system are far greater than at any other time in our history. We are challenged by the ability to fill young minds with information, whilst preparing them to cope with dramatically changing social dynamics in the world at large.

Within this environment of upheaval, education can only evolve if it is allowed to develop and function without heed to the narrow confines of current political or corporate influence that comes with growing corporate sponsorship.

Only then can it be free to focus upon a deeper understanding of how best to support, encourage and nurture our children to take up their common role as the future Creators of Life.

I would argue that our Evolution to a multicultural Society, and the growing impact of modern technology opening up every aspect of our lives, has changed forever the traditional educational models we have previously operated.

In Korea, for example, youngsters are on the Web all the time and now showing signs of greater levels of intelligence in their ability to *assimilate information*. Having an outline understanding of the basic subjects is sufficient for them to then expand upon this in later life, if the curiosity takes them.

No subject is a taboo anymore, and this freedom of information places a new pressure upon both parents and the educational process, in forging and maintaining close links with the faster pace of personal development the young are now experiencing.

The Times They Are a Changing

The days of giving the establishment perspective on Life are fast receding, as traditional boundaries break down. As a result, a greater freedom of information allows the young to shape their own perspective on Life, and the Society they will eventually be contributing to.

The nature of this challenge can best be illustrated by the many religious beliefs that have rationalised our experiences of Life, and have been the bedrock of traditional educational training.

Traditionally, the delivery of these wisdoms has always directed the manner in which we interact with each other. The intensity and diversity of views propounded have constantly caused widespread separation and conflict within our species throughout our history, as differing factions use these beliefs as the source of their power bases.

> *Do not train children in learning by force and harshness, but direct them to it by what amuses their minds, so that you may be better able to discover with accuracy the peculiar bent of the genius of each.*
>
> PLATO

Our current Evolutionary progress is now dictating the need for a more balanced perspective that nurtures unification, rather than separation, in religious belief. The challenge for our future education systems is to support this and all other uniting beliefs, whilst providing students with the ability to think more laterally and better manage the vast amounts of information they now have access to in this new environment.

Speaking from personal experience, there is a desperate need, in a rapidly changing environment, for support in assessing and determining how young people reach an informed philosophy of their own from the vast, uncensored databanks available – be it a single faith philosophy or otherwise.

Present Society might be very uncomfortable with providing this level of freedom of thought to the young, no matter what the subject, because there appears to be little control over the beliefs they might formulate. Although there is not much that can be done about it, I believe it is to be nurtured and encouraged.

The traditional barriers of separation, whether religious, political or racial, can no longer be sustained within a growing multicultural Society. The social networking sites like Facebook and YouTube provide a sense of international unity between members, whilst also allowing those members to maintain their essential and intrinsic individuality.

> *As the Internet submits its vast databanks to all humanity, it assists with the cohesion of the new global Society, by providing a common library from which the young may shape their own beliefs.* JTC

This new unifying environment can only support parents and the education system, whatever their location or ethnicity, in working with their charges in how they manage this emerging era of unlimited and uncensored information.

The Real Challenge we Face

The real challenge, of Herculean proportions, is returning the authority to both parents and educational staff to carry out their traditional duties. We know from experience that this is the only means by which the young can learn and experience the boundaries they need to adopt if they are to become members and contribute to a healthily functioning Society.

I am of the belief that there is a correlation between the reduction of parent/teacher authority and the rise in anti-social behaviour over the last decade or so, as we deny the truth of how we function as a species.

To emphasise this point, in 2011 British cities were subjected to a wave of rioting by youths who showed no respect towards the members of their communities or their property. Video clips were witness to youngsters laughing as sole trader shops burned furiously.

This heartless reaction is indicative of a youth demonstrating a complete ignorance of personal and social boundaries that define moral responsibility. One young rioter, when asked what, in his opinion, would have stopped the riots, gave a simple three-word answer: 'Jobs and discipline'.

The profound wisdom in this simple observation is overwhelming, and strikes at the very heart of how we perceive our support for the young in this 21st century.

Obsessed with the need to *financialise* our education system, whilst also giving our children human rights beyond their comprehension and capabilities, we have ignored their fundamental need to rebel, as they constantly test the boundaries of human interaction and establish their own identity.

This need to rebel, and the means to manage that rebellion, has been an intrinsic part of who and what we are since time immemorial. It provides our young with the valuable lessons they need to learn about the moral standards by which Society functions, resulting in a respect for their community and the outside world.

Nowhere are these characteristics more evident than when a number of Society's most *difficult* youngsters experience a few days on ocean-going sailing ships. After their time on these Tall Ships, many return completely changed and with a new respect that has come out of their meeting with the forces of Nature. Finding that they are completely unable to retaliate against this omnipotent force, they learn respect from having met the ultimate boundary.

I have touched on this subject in a previous chapter, and it is so critically important that it bears repeating here. We are designed as a species to continually push the boundaries and strive *throughout our lives*, and rebellion is a part of this striving.

Through rebellion we learn about integrity, the unwritten moral code that differentiates between acceptable and unacceptable behaviour towards each other in every sphere of Life.

(It was this unwritten code by which Society determined the actions of bankers and politicians as immoral and unacceptable after the 2007/8 financial crisis, evidenced by a growing anger and loss of respect for both institutions. It became obvious that 'Free' markets of any description can only work in our best interests when supported by integrity and effective boundaries.)

Awareness of this code emerges during our formative years and returns us to the need to restore the authority to teachers and parents as they work to imbue the young with a sense of integrity and responsibility.

This facet of their education has huge implications on how future Society is shaped. In focussing upon how our young people assume responsibility for their own actions, we are developing a mind-set of respect and responsibility in them that ripples across all aspects of Life.

> *We are all managers of this Planet and need to learn respect for that which provides all of our needs. Only by starting with the young can we change our current self-destructive beliefs and produce a sustainable world.* JTC

In this manner, we are not only sowing seeds that will influence the positive future interaction of our species, thereby reducing the constant conflict that has contributed to the dark side of our history, but also encouraging greater responsibility in the management of this Planet. This would be passed on to future generations through a gradually evolving philosophy.

Encouraging our children's education in this manner will sow the seeds of new belief patterns that would replace the immediacy of current short-term thinking. This would also contribute to an expansion in our current traditional beliefs about the purpose of Life, resonating more deeply with who and what we are as a species.

Within this same expansion of belief lies the need to provide greater levels of support to the young when they have completed their formal education.

It Doesn't Finish with their Schooling

Given that the educational environment is all they have known whilst growing from children to young adults, there is little effective support for their transition from academic life to the outside world. This is one of the most critical stages in any young person's life, as they prepare to stand on their own two feet and begin assuming the wider responsibilities of adulthood.

Introducing them to that adult world within a *controlled* environment would allow them to experience Life from perspectives they have not previously confronted. The onus would be upon them to fend for themselves in keeping mind, body and spirit together, whilst acting with integrity, discipline and initiative in all that they are challenged to face.

In the UK, *Conscription* was something that took young people into the armed forces for two years, after they had left the education process. During this time, they had to get on with complete strangers, support and nurture themselves through a pride in personal appearance, discipline and extensive application of personal initiative.

Conscription ended in the 1950s. I am unaware of anyone who did not speak of the experience with other than fond affection and respect for the values it taught, which supported them through the rest of their lives.

It bolstered self-esteem and gave them a confidence to go out into Society and make their contribution, prepared at all times to take total responsibility for their actions.

To my mind, this form of preparation is indicative of a Society that is not only committed to the proper nurture of its young, but also acknowledges the need to take full responsibility for the future of Life on this beautiful Planet.

Finally, we also need to recognise that education is not a *business* but a *vocational* activity. People do not become teachers to make large amounts of money. Children do not become educated within time frames, or as units of learning.

We are talking about the process by which each individual has the best possible opportunity to reach their fullest potential, with or without examination awards, and in so doing becoming a positive contributor to Society. (Winston Churchill, my lifetime hero and, like me, a poor-academic, went on to become one of our greatest leaders, famed around the world.)

Our Young Are Like The Soil In Our Garden

It doesn't matter how we design our garden – it could be all grass, all trees, all plants, all vegetables or a combination of each – the soil in which they are planted is not concerned. It will grow whatever we provide it with. Likewise, whatever we choose to plant in our children's young minds will also grow and flower as the next Society.

Religions have always been aware of this characteristic of our species and have used it to further their own agendas, resulting in the constant religious power conflicts that have dogged our species for millennia.

In this 21st century, saddling the young with debt they had no part in creating will not breed consumers, but rebellion against beliefs that restrict them from living their lives to the full. In America, we are now seeing constant atrocities with guns and bombs by mainly young people. Is this because of feelings of anger and frustration of monumental proportions, as they view their bleak futures in the political and economic climate our beliefs have now created?

Remember, that out of the battlefields of Lebanon grew the powerful resistance movement Hezbollah, with its expanding power and political influence committed to remedying the abuses of the past. Although their support of the Assad regime is now losing them support, it in no way diminishes the type of environment in which new powerful groups are born.

What we sow we reap, and we cannot hide from this aspect of how we function. This is an awesome responsibility we have yet to fully recognise, and why our children's education must always be sacrosanct.

When we do recognise this fact, we will also come to realise that, within our children's education resides the catalyst for World Peace ... and nowhere else.
JTC

Greater Understanding Defines our Rights and Responsibilities

If education is the means by which we attain greater personal freedom, then there is a need to place personal responsibility at the forefront of this process. It is one of Life's many paradoxes, that the greater the freedom the greater the responsibility, and is something we ignore at our peril.

The Human Rights legislation was conceived to address the often barbaric manner in which many sectors of our species have been treated over the millennia, seeking to successfully support their gradual emancipation and empowerment.

However, in those countries, where human abuse is not excessive, the very legislation itself is being abused. It seems to me as though we are having a similar experience to Prohibition in America, where good intention backfired upon the Society that introduced it.

When the American government gave in to the anti-alcohol lobby, human nature was completely overlooked, in a seemingly well-meaning attempt at improving Society. The legacy of Prohibition has been the emergence of the most sophisticated crime network the world has ever seen – something that this well-meaning lobby neither wanted, nor envisioned.

> *No amount of legislation, no matter how well-meaning, can replace human compassion.* JTC

Human Rights legislation has been in force for some time now. It is also becoming apparent that we might need to address its present singular application to the human condition by evolving an equal, and essentially balancing, emphasis upon human *responsibilities*. This omission, in the past, has now become the source of a growing challenge to our freedoms as a Society, creating separation and conflict in communities large and small, instead of unifying them.

Vast networks of businesses have mushroomed to reap profit from the tiniest infringement of one person's *Rights* by another individual or organisation. This profit-seeking frenzy of financial compensation from human fallibility is turning citizen against citizen, whilst constantly threatening and reducing the services and facilities we have traditionally enjoyed.

From children's playgrounds to amusement parks, and from medical advice centres to traditional educational establishments, nothing is sacrosanct. In our endeavours to assert our rights to compensation from Life's inherent risks, we have also embarked upon a futile attempt to remove all risk from Life, which is something I personally believe is not conducive to the human condition.

Human Rights and the Benefits System

In Britain, as in other countries, there is a welfare system that has been in place for many years. It is not a new concept and can be traced as far back as the Roman Empire, with the introduction of a welfare programme, *Alimenta,* by the emperor Trajan during the 1st century.

This legislation, like the Human Rights legislation, was designed to protect and empower those members of Society that might be placed at a disadvantage by what Life has to offer. Human Rights and the welfare system, as separate pieces of legislation of empowerment, are a tribute to our compassion as a species.

> *No man is above the law and no man below it.*
>
> THEODORE ROOSEVELT

However, when we combine these two worthy pieces of legislation, their ability to empower becomes a double-edged sword. In what is now described as a *Benefits culture,* we exercise our right to demand State benefits, rather than our right to *call upon them when we have exhausted every other responsible course of action available to us.*

It is here that what I like to call the *Prohibition Factor* comes into play, as the well-intentioned actions introduced for the good of Society increasingly backfire upon that Society. Human fallibility enters the equation, as the less scrupulous see the opportunities to freeload from the responsible actions of their own Society.

Teenage pregnancies have escalated as the young are driven by our most primeval urge to indulge in the enjoyment, without taking up the responsibility that comes with the aftermath of unprotected sex.

Whilst it is accepted that some youngsters will take responsibility for their actions, the majority will not, and the young mother, often urged on by her parent(s), will come to expect the state to feed, clothe and shelter her and her child.

We cannot ignore the need for support of the young in this scenario, but this has evolved into an understanding that there is a *Right* to do whatever we please, and Society has to pick up the pieces (and the cost) when things go wrong.

It is here that we need greater social cohesion, by encouraging personal responsibilities that complement legislated rights. To recognise, for example, that benefits have always been the safety net *when all other responsible action has failed.*

The problem is now becoming acute, both morally and financially, as third generation families are entering a benefits regime they truly believe they have a right to enjoy.

My son, in his short period between jobs, witnessed an attempted assault upon a benefits clerk because she would not agree to pay benefit to a young man who had made no attempt to find work since his last visit to the employment centre.

This is not an isolated incident, born witness to by the need for security guards at many of these establishments. It demonstrates how an originally good intention can backfire upon a Society endeavouring to be responsible, when that ethos of responsibility is not reciprocated by those benefitting from that good intention.

Our Rights are not Negotiable ... But Maybe How we Get Them Is

The *Prohibition Factor* defines our abilities and fallibilities when we seek to improve our overall quality of Life. The freedom to access anything such as alcohol and *free* benefit money comes at a price, and that price is our personal responsibility in how we use them.

> *Whenever I hear anyone arguing for slavery, I feel a strong impulse to see it tried on him personally.*
>
> ABRAHAM LINCOLN

(I accept that the economic climate since 2007/8 is exacerbating the problem as I write, but I am focussing upon the culture and not the cause.)

The current imbalance in Human Rights legislation is having a devastating impact upon the young (in addition to unwanted pregnancies), which is also bearing down on Society in general. As covered earlier, time and again we hear of cases where respect for adult authority in the exercise of its duties, particularly in the parenting and educational environments, is being jeopardised.

To counter this rupture in our struggle for a cohesive Society, it might be in the best interests of all concerned if the full spectrum of human rights is passed to them gradually, with a full inheritance of those rights at a particular level of maturity – perhaps when the age of majority (18 in the UK) has been reached.

In this way, they could be motivated to strive for this important acknowledgment of their attainment of majority, by their conduct and manner towards Society during the intervening years. Attaining majority would become an even more important landmark in their journey through Life, with their entry into Society as a fully-contributing (and benefitting) member.

The true value and importance of this personal attainment might be underwritten from an understanding that all or some of the rights could be reviewed if they perpetrated abuses against Society – elevating further the importance of Society in a rapidly changing world.

We are in bondage to the law in order that we may be free.

CICERO

By better understanding who and what we are, we are better placed to expand present important legislation. This is not only to protect people, but to prepare and motivate them from a young age to want to play a responsible part in contributing to the Life we create.

If a precedent is required for this preparation in order to assume responsibility for the full panoply of Human Rights, we might consider our attitude to driving. Here, we understand the devastation the young can do if allowed unbridled access to motor vehicles, be they cars of motorbikes.

We train them and we test them – often, more than once – and finally allow them into Society. Insurance companies will bear witness, in their premium rates, to the high risks that young qualified drivers can present to Society in their impetuous behaviour, as they seek to find the boundaries of their driving skills – a true acknowledgment of the human condition.

Why, therefore, should we be any the less responsible in how we prepare our young to conduct themselves for our collective benefit within Society? By placing a greater emphasis upon the attainment of human rights, rather than an automatic entry to their benefits, which seriously devalues them, we also work in tandem with our need to strive as a species.

The Ripple Effect

Of equal importance, to my mind, is the vast ripple effect the subject of responsibility has upon our relationships, not only with each other, but also with the Planet and all the other inhabitants.

At a time when we are becoming increasingly concerned with our Planet's ability to replace all we are now capable of *vacuuming up* from her surface, be it on the land or in the sea, I don't believe it unreasonable to question just how responsible we are in the wider arena of Life.

I hear and I forget. I see and I remember. I do and I understand.

CONFUCIUS

If we begin with our attitude to the Planet's other inhabitants, several decades ago the whale became an endangered species because of their irresponsible slaughter by us. All of the campaigning and other charitable endeavours had little effect in curtailing this activity, until people were taken out to observe these beautiful creatures in their own habitat.

Almost overnight the climate changed, ignorance was dispelled and a new respect was born that introduced legislation to more *responsibly* manage how they were hunted.

This technique, learnt from a better understanding of how we function, is now being applied to many other endangered species, reversing declining numbers by eliciting greater responsibility and compassion from us.

In spite of this successful formula, we continue to introduce well-intended legislation that sometimes loses sight of this bigger picture, resulting in Society scoring an *own goal* that inhibits tried and tested good work. This was graphically demonstrated to me during a visit to a wildlife park devoted to saving the cheetah, whose numbers are now down to just 2,000 and falling.

The sanctuary had two of these magnificent animals, one of which had been hand-reared by the staff and was, therefore, not afraid to make public appearances. I was told that these cats would not attack humans in their natural environment, but rather run away when confronted.

Because of this, the park was able to demonstrate the cheetah's awesome speed directly in front of visitors, by having it chase a dead rabbit, pulled behind a Land Rover at speeds of up to 70 miles per hour, with only a safety leash attached to a high wire.

This spectacular sight got close to replicating the dynamics of this wild animal without danger to those watching, because of the cat's nature and the safety precautions designed by world experts. Here, we see another excellent example of our experiences with whales being replicated.

Where does all of this fit in with Human Rights and Responsibilities?

In this case, the local authority, within whose jurisdiction the park fell, was anxious not to be the subject of a claim for injury in these financially restricting times. Rather than encouraging the maintenance of professionally engineered safety precautions, it sought to ban the event on grounds of *health and safety* legislation.

This piece of legislation has been spawned by Human Rights law to protect large organisations from lawsuits by individuals or groups who, for the large part, seem either incapable or unwilling to take adequate responsibility for their own actions. In this case, the choice of whether to attend the sanctuary or not.

Here, we can see that the imbalance between our rights and responsibilities is restricting a greater understanding of the natural world, through a tried and tested means of education that recognises how we function, and could have an impact upon the future survival of these magnificent creatures.

Denying more and more of the facilities and services we create before we have decided whether they benefit us or not, because of legislation that needs more attention, represents, in my opinion, a *Prohibition Factor* of monumental proportions.

How do We Introduce Balance?

In defining the primary responsibilities we need to consider, to try and bring balance to current Human Rights legislation, it would seem prudent to understand how we perceive the basic functioning of Society. A good place to start would be with the 10 Commandments, or similar ancient and proven wisdom.

In February 2005, Channel 4 in Britain conducted a poll to establish how people would update the traditional Christian 10 Commandments to operate in a modern world. This is the result:

1. Treat others as you would want them to treat you. *(Overwhelmingly)*
2. Take responsibility for your actions.
3. Do not kill.
4. Be honest.
5. Do not steal.
6. Protect and nurture children.
7. Protect the environment.
8. Look after the vulnerable.
9. Never be violent.
10. Protect your family.

This poll not only serves to illustrate the need to update traditional beliefs, but also acts as a yardstick as to how we perceive moral values in this 21st century. Perhaps this offers a suitable benchmark from which to begin the construction of Human *Responsibilities* legislation.

The greatest sadness to me in all of this is that current dominant thinking seems to restrict us from assuming greater responsibility for our actions. The 'nanny state' is certainly justifying the work of our parliaments, but it is effectively denying us the opportunity to build and develop our own character and personal strengths as individuals and a species. Continually passing the blame to another is not only denying us the ability to build and strengthen character, but also converting us into a species of victims, and we are the poorer for that.

Only by better understanding who and what we are about and how we function as a species can we then create meaningful boundaries. These boundaries will nurture and support the improvement of the human condition, breeding higher levels of respect and self-esteem across the whole panoply of services and interactions within Society.

Defining Life – Science, Religion and the Third Way

Science and Religion are the two primary belief systems we have created to define our place in the *grand scheme of things* and help us to better understand what Life is all about. It is also no coincidence that these beliefs specifically address our 'left' (Logical) and 'right' (Intuitive) brain in directing our powers of perception.

We are often aware of the contest that goes on in our own head between our left and right brain activity. This happens when we *feel* that the *logical answer* to a problem doesn't somehow seem comfortable – or the solution that *feels* comfortable just isn't *logical*.

The complex task of working out what Life is all about, from the conflicting messages we get from both sides of our brain, is further exacerbated by the conflicting messages we get from both of our primary belief systems as they, too, contest with each other for a dominant position in Society.

The competing perspectives of left and right brain manifest in all forms of human activity that seek answers, from personal challenges to debate forums and even public interviews. It is in the very act of contesting that we bring meaning and substance to the answers we eventually get, or not!

It is worth, therefore, entering into debate now to see if we can find answers to this perpetual conflict that will improve our overall quality of Life.

The Case for Science

This view of Life specifies that wisdom is based upon facts that have to be seen, touched and proven. Scientific wisdom can best be identified by one of its most pre-eminent members, Charles Darwin, who postulated that Life was not created but is an Evolutionary process, driven by the natural selection of the species, something completely opposed by religion.

Over the millennia, the freedom enjoyed by science to constantly venture into uncharted waters has been responsible for the stratospheric growth in our technological capabilities. In my lifetime, I have experienced our daily milk delivery by horse and cart as a child and watched, a few decades later, as scientists placed a laser beam of light on the surface of the moon.

Medical science has astounded us as new cures are found for ailments thought incurable and enabled the human lifespan to double in just a few short centuries. Neurosurgery has taken us to depths of understanding about the workings of our body and discovered cures to repair it that would have been deemed impossible in the last century.

Contraception has reached a level of sophistication now that has become a double-edged sword. On the one hand, we can confidently plan the size of our family, although there are questions as to whether this development has also been responsible for the decline in moral standards within Society.

Science, therefore, has been the biggest contributor to our development as a species and the manner in which we live Life on this Planet.

The Case for Religion

Traditional religious belief offers the understanding that Life was *created* by an unseen deity, and that we are all responsible to this deity for every aspect of how we live our lives. Our actions are regulated by Commandments that dictate whether we are *good* or *bad*, with the certainty of divine retribution for any past and present transgressions.

Throughout our history, the majority of our species have been content to have their lives directed by *faith without proof* in adopting one or more of the many religious beliefs that flourish across the globe to meet our diverse needs as a species.

Indeed, some famous names within the scientific community have acknowledged the presence of *intelligence* at work in the universe, including Isaac Newton, the father of modern science, and Albert Einstein. However, this has never brought about a thawing of relations between the two institutions.

As a species we have always needed the succour of our religious doctrines in times of trouble when our personal world has fallen apart. Life challenges us repeatedly, and it is within the religious books of wisdom that answers have often been found that return our confidence and self-esteem, enabling us to go back into the world and pick our lives up again.

Religion, therefore, has been the 'rock' that gives direction to how we manage our lives and the values we adopt within Society.

... And the Problem They Both Present Us With

What seems a paradox of monumental proportions to me is that both Religion and Science, as the primary directors of how we perceive Life, share one common feature – a lack of direct accountability for their teachings and beliefs about Life.

Religion passes responsibility for its directives to an all-seeing deity, supported by such phrases as *it is the will of God* or *God is on our side.*

This lack of accountability is justified by religious institutions in a blind adherence to beliefs dating back to a time when women were perceived as little more than goods or chattels. In this 21st century, the continued inability of these institutions to champion the cause of equality for women is one of many factors that increasingly question the credibility of traditional religious belief, as we evolve as a species.

I attribute my success to this – I never gave or took any excuses.

FLORENCE NIGHTINGALE, 1820–1910

Shifting the blame to a *deity* in order to protect us from our own irresponsible actions may have worked, up to a point, when we were contained rural communities. Globalisation, however, is already demonstrating the failing influence these beliefs are able to exert to adequately address the traditional lack of human integrity and respect we have for our fellow inhabitants.

Science, on the other hand, deals in the quantifiable evidence obtained from experimentation and, as such, *the morality of its findings does not enter the scientific process.* This responsibility is passed back to their employers, who represent our two main purveyors of vested interest – the political and corporate sectors.

Science is the great antidote to the poison of enthusiasm and superstition.

ADAM SMITH, THE WEALTH OF NATIONS, 1776

In the case of scientific process, this lack of accountability is a positive feature, allowing nothing to inhibit its ability to investigate all aspects of Life. However, its relationship with its employers is an uneasy one in how that knowledge is subsequently applied.

This is particularly pertinent when we consider, for example, the ramifications of the discovery of nuclear energy. The political will that was the motivation behind making *the bomb* has now placed a dark cloud over all humanity, with its awesome potential for global devastation.

Indeed, the very scientists responsible for the development of the atomic bomb subsequently became its greatest opponents. Robert Oppenheimer, who directed the development of this awesome weapon, reportedly said later that in its moment of activation a phrase from the Bhagavad Gita came to mind – *"I am become death, destroyer of worlds"*. Source: Wikipedia.

In the blame game for our current state of affairs as a species, there are those who might argue that Religion is not responsible for Global Warming, and neither is Science responsible for continuous human conflict. They have however, each played a part through their actions and beliefs, supported by a mutual lack of institutional accountability that renders these arguments difficult to accept.

Religion has remained transfixed by unchanging beliefs that have not enabled our personal growth to keep pace with scientific achievement.

I believe that this lack of parallel development in our thinking about what Life is all about has resulted in a widening gap between what we create and how we responsibly manage it – be it financial instruments or instruments of war.

Science does not know its debt to imagination.

RALPH WALDO EMERSON

If you look at the growing sophistication in the destructive capabilities of our weaponry over time – from the bow and arrow to laser-guided bombs – it is astounding. However, unchanging moral values have seen rape become a *weapon* of war as we continue a historic lack of respect for the female of the species.

Our ability, therefore, to responsibly manage what we create is seriously impeded – be it financial instruments or instruments of warfare. JTC

With the rush now on to secure the Planet's remaining energy resources, whilst trying to deal with growing global debt, and religious extremism pursuing the eternal myth of world domination, we risk our destruction as a species if we are unable to defuse or effectively manage these 21st century values.

Over time, both institutions have seen it necessary to become embroiled in the political arena to support and further their own interests, resulting in vested interest increasingly holding sway over much of what they do.

This has produced another paradox of global proportions. Institutions that should be providing our most enlightened thinking have become responsible for the continued imbalance in our development as a species as they vie for positions of dominance over Society's values.

Men are probably nearer the central truth in their superstitions than in their science.

HENRY DAVID THOREAU

Psychology Could Offer the Solution with a Third Way

If the imbalances caused by our two primary belief systems are contributing to the challenges we now face in our inability to manage what we create, Einstein would again argue that, as part of the problem, they are incapable of providing a solution.

It is here, I believe, that psychology has an important contribution to make. If we return to the subject of our left and right brains, most of our personal turmoil comes from the conflict between these two aspects of who and what we are.

Over time, we have come to learn much about the functioning of this aspect of human behaviour and how to resolve it, and any other conflict for that matter, by getting both sides working together and supporting each other.

A science-based *Moral Code* could achieve this merging by offering a combined understanding of the forces at work in Life. This third way combines scientific and religious practices that identify *what is working* and remedy *what is not working* in our relationships with each other and the Planet, replacing traditional subjective and confrontational judgements of *Right & Wrong*.

By identifying known characteristics about how we and the Natural world function, we can become aware of natural disciplines and influences affecting our day to day lives, something that has always been an intrinsic part of Life.

There are powerful *Life forces* at work. Balance and Change come immediately to mind which, like Integrity, we currently pay scant regard to. However, because of how we function, they exert a powerful impact upon our day-to-day lives.

Understanding and respecting these forces becomes possible by combining quantifiable scientific observation and religious belief within a unifying framework that identifies these powerful forces and their far-reaching impact upon the human condition.

Building bridges between these traditionally opposing beliefs, I believe, broadens and strengthens each of them. This ensures they continue to police, probe and question each other's direction, as well as our own development.

> *Faith is to believe what we do not see; and the reward of this faith is to see what we believe.*
>
> SAINT AURELIUS AUGUSTINE, AD 354–430

The scope of Scientific application might be broadened, as is happening with quantum physics, through accepting the presence of *that which cannot be measured*, attributing its application to known and quantifiable aspects of both the human condition and the universe at large.

Traditional Religious thinking may similarly broaden its base by acknowledging the need to constantly update and adapt the moral code of a continuously evolving Society.

We already know that we are better able to take control of our personal lives when we get the left and right sides of our brain working together. Indeed, science is now of the opinion that there are elements of the left side in the right side and vice versa, supporting a greater merging of what was previously seen as opposing forces.

No longer would we continue to fight about our perceptions of Life, something that has caused our Evolution to be a constant and painful struggle, but rather take direct control of the process. With a better understanding of how it functions, we can work with it, achieving a level of responsibility and self-empowerment for our species that has never before been dreamt of.

The True Empowerment of Women is Essential to our Future

She avoids aggression

Elinor Gadon PhD, an American cultural historian, author and academic, makes the point that, in recent archaeological research, there is no sign of warfare in any Neolithic Goddess cultures, as there is no evidence of fortifications, violent death, invasion or conquest. Perhaps this is why it is postulated that women would never send their children to war! JTC

This chapter has much in common with the previous chapter in dealing with our integration as a species. In Jungian psychology, the anima and animus represent the masculine and feminine characteristics of the unconscious – true inner self – in every one of us.

The trick, we are told, to becoming a balanced person, capable of taking full advantage of what Life has to offer, is to get these two aspects working in balance with each other – in a similar fashion to left and right brain activity.

From this basic understanding of how we function, it follows that there is a duty upon us to ensure that both the male and female of our species are also working in equal balance and harmony with each other, for our long-term benefit.

Let me also emphasise at the outset that, when I refer to balance, I do not suggest for one moment that women have to mirror what men do to achieve equality. Balance, for me, can only ever mean that there is an equal application of power and perspective from women, in this thing called Life, as that which has traditionally been exerted by their male counterparts.

The current imbalance has been with us since we were cave-dwellers and has seriously affected our ability to balance our development as a species. It is like a Greek galley, with all of the rowers on one side being made incapable of making their contribution to the ship's progress. In this state, the galley will only ever travel in endless circles, experiencing the same restricted journey and making it incapable of achieving its true potential.

From the cartoon images of cavemen dragging women by the hair, to the modern-day atrocities of rape as a weapon of war, men have dominated Life on Planet Earth through their physical strength – no more, no less.

I believe that this gender imbalance has also contributed to our constant conflict over the millennia, as the testosterone-driven male ego functions across the broad spectrum of activities of our species. Please remember, this is an observation and not a criticism, as the subject matter is far too important ... and, after all, I too am a man!

The answer to many of the dilemmas faced by Society today could be found in a better understanding of the human condition. JTC

If we step back and look at the contribution women have been allowed to play in our Evolution as a species, we will see it has moved from *derisory* to *limited but growing*. This imbalance in our overall development has been held in check by the influence of our traditional institutions, including those responsible for our moral wellbeing, as they continue to diligently resist full gender equality.

I believe, however, that we are now reaching a point where the huge Evolutionary changes going on are beginning to weaken that traditional thinking, and will eventually bring about the balancing of gender that is so essential to our future survival as a species.

It is here that I see one of the clearest examples of the need for us to better understand who and what we are about. With this heightened awareness, we can consciously begin to manage the Evolutionary process by integrating the very special talents women have to offer.

From the beginning of time, men have had the skills to *provide* and women the skills to *sustain*. Going back to our caveman, we see Life at its simplest as the male put the food on the table and the female saw to the critical reproduction and maintenance of our species.

What seems patently obvious to me, with the problems we are now facing, is masculine-driven short-term thinking – and here, profit is very much a masculine value in its demand for instant gratification. We are constantly inventing new ways of providing, be it financial instruments or decimation of this Planet's resources, but the feminine energy, force and concentration necessary to SUSTAIN what we are doing is non-existent.

This suicidal pattern will never resolve itself until such time as we recognise the essential and critical contribution women must now make, calling a halt to our historic spiral of constant conflict and self-destruction as a species.

On 1 February 2010, Pope Benedict XVI deplored the effects of equal rights legislation in the UK on the grounds that it imposes limitations upon religious organisations on how they administer their beliefs.

SOURCE: OPENDEMOCRACY.NET

In our most important areas of Life, we have introduced legislation to stop monopolies of corporate activity because, here, we understand that domination in any sector only benefits the dominant. Yet, we continue to operate one of the biggest monopolies in our history to our own detriment, by suppressing a full and equal female contribution to our Evolutionary process.

In those areas where women have reached positions of power, it has been because they have applied themselves with far greater diligence than their male counterparts, often suffering harassment and sexual abuse as a by-product of the process. Just imagine how our world will change when this tenacity is harnessed for our collective benefit.

> *'One of my dreams has come true: half the cabinet seats are held by women,' said the Bolivian president. 'The new cabinet is made up of singers, lawyers, economists, caucus leaders, doctors and workers... for the first time in the history of Bolivia a woman is head of the Labour Affairs Ministry.'*
>
> MERCO PRESS, 25 JANUARY 2010

I would suggest that it is also important to recognise that women should not try to compete with men by playing them at their own game. That would mean that the game would not change, and we would be no further forward as a species.

The task before women now, as I see it, is to play their own game *in the same arena*, bringing new values and perspectives that are truly feminine, thereby introducing a greater balance to Society's values.

Let's face it, there are plenty of opportunities for women to bring their special talents to the struggling arenas of media, banking and politics, where the public are increasingly demanding greater transparency and respect towards the 99%.

There is not an area of Life that would not change for the better, as this feminine influence spreads across the globe. Just consider the impact upon extremism, be it political, corporate or religious, as the current perspectives are reconsidered from a more balanced viewpoint.

> *'Why should we pay taxes when we have no part in the honours, the commands, the state craft for which you contend?'*
>
> HORTENSIA, SPEECH BEFORE THE ROMAN TRIUMVIRATE, ITALY, 42 BC

In this 21st century, we are seeing the emergence of a more balanced Society in some areas of our Planet as women take their rightful place alongside the men, but it is painfully slow. This true unity has already taken place in Bolivia in January 2010, when 50 per cent of the cabinet ministers appointed were women.

Whilst it is not the province of this book to become embroiled in the politics of any country or party, perhaps this development has grown out of the country's recent history, that has seen a total of 193 coups d'état, averaging a change of government once every ten months.

For me, redressing the imbalance of gender in this violent country will offer the first ever opportunity for women to play a critical role in changing the traditional political and environmental landscapes.

I would further venture that, *provided they have been fully empowered,* this new feminine influence will lead to a calming of the continuous conflict experienced by Bolivia's people. I would also stick my neck out by suggesting this could happen within decades rather than centuries.

The same is apparent in India where, in March 2010, the Indian upper parliament passed a historic affirmative-action bill that would reserve 33 per cent of all parliamentary seats for women.

This initiative was driven by the frustration felt by Indian women over their subservient position in Society. This frustration has caused the manifestation of the *gulabi,* or *pink gangs* (because of their hot-pink sari *uniforms*) operating in the Bundelkhand district of the Uttar Pradesh state, one of the poorest districts of India.

This movement was founded by a fearless 40-year-old woman, Sampat Pal Devi. Her childhood upbringing and marriage at 12, with five children by the age of 15, is behind what has been described as a mini revolution on behalf of women, by looking out for victims of abuse.

These gangs pay visits to abusive husbands to demand they stop beating their wives. If these demands are ignored, the gangs return with bamboo sticks and *negotiate* a cessation to the violence. Pal admits she does not always use the stick, *but it helps change the mind of men who think they are more powerful than her.*

The gulabi group now has tens of thousands of members, including male supporters. From a personal perspective, I wonder if this growth points to a grassroots raising of self-esteem amongst Indian women, who now want to respond to the age-old problems they have faced of honor killings, dowries, child marriages, and female feticide.

> *New beliefs are necessary when we become out of balance with this Planet and each other. We make mistakes – of course we do. It is never what happens that is important, but how we deal with it – Always!* JTC

Whilst this type of vigilante action needs to convert into an acknowledged political cause for its further development, it meets an immediate and growing global frustration and need that has never been expressed so extensively since the Suffragette movement at the beginning of the 20th century.

Turning our attention now to the commercial environment, there is an even more exciting development at work, endorsing my earlier comment about the feminine contribution so necessary to present-day male values. This can only accelerate the true empowerment of women, by dramatically influencing the traditional financial environment, whilst taking Society's values in a whole new direction.

> *'Women have the right to mount the scaffold; they should likewise have the right to mount the rostrum.'*
>
> OLYMPE DE GOUGES, AUTHOR OF DECLARATION OF RIGHTS OF WOMEN, FRANCE, 1791

Jessica Jackley, co-founder of Kiva.org, has harnessed the web to introduce one of the world's first peer-to-peer micro-lending platforms. Since its launch in 2005, Kiva has facilitated over $490M in loans, connecting lenders and entrepreneurs around the world.

I have deliberately put in bold the empowering words that follow, to highlight the exciting way forward this organisation has taken in its thinking about lending and finance which, I am sure, comes with a feminine perspective.

By seeking to create *relationships beyond financial transactions,* building *partnership relationships – characterised by mutual dignity and respect,* it is supporting our growing natural unification as a species within the new global environment.

This last point is absolutely critical in supporting my argument about the equal contribution women have to, and must make, in Society. The thinking behind the work of Kiva.org goes beyond profit and competition by understanding, from a female perspective, who and what we are as a species.

Indeed, this new-style corporate ethos, applied not only to the poor but also to small businesses, and all the other areas that are not fully supported by the traditional banking system, offer vast opportunities of specialist activity and empowerment for women.

The future growth of this *enlightened* Banking will, I am certain, be recognised for its skills and humanitarian philosophy. Not only is it supporting the poor, but also motivating and supporting communities to financially contribute to local small businesses and entrepreneurs, thus benefitting from their subsequent successes in the future.

> *Kiva's mission is to connect people, through lending, for the sake of alleviating poverty and was born of the following beliefs:*
>
> ***The poor are highly motivated*** *and can be very successful when given an opportunity.*
>
> ***By connecting people we can create relationships beyond financial transactions,*** *and build a global community expressing support and encouragement of one another.*

Kiva promotes:

Dignity: *Kiva encourages partnership relationships as opposed to benefactor relationships. Partnership relationships are characterised by mutual dignity and respect.*

Accountability: *Loans encourage more accountability than donations where repayment is not expected.*

Transparency: *The Kiva website is an open platform where communication can flow freely around the world.*

SOURCE: WWW.KIVA.ORG

This concept is again being pursued by Jessica Jackley in another of her ventures with Profounder (www.profounder.com), with the unique strapline *crowdfunding for your business.* Once again, her philosophy has a uniting influence, with the wider implications this invaluable support can provide in rebuilding fragmented communities.

I believe that this constant suppression of an equal contribution by women to Life on Planet Earth is driven by a fear that women will dominate and run things in the same way men have. This is simply not possible because of the point I made earlier, which is that women have a different perspective on Life.

This difference translates into being less confrontational and more compassionate – the primary needs for resolving the problems we are currently facing. These qualities can only ensure a greater balance to our future Evolution.

This difference in attitude can again be seen in Iceland, where two women set up a new financial services business in 2007, and survived the financial Armageddon in their country a year later. Halla Tómasdóttir and Kristín Pétursdóttir steered Audur Capital through the financial storm with *five feminine values* that directed the financial services their company provided. These values are:

a) Independence in thinking and operating to be able to put their clients' interests first and not be compromised.

b) Risk Awareness. That they only invested in what they understand (as opposed to the sub-prime mortgage market promoted by their male counterparts and which *nobody* understood).

c) Straight Talking. Where the downside of the risk is brought into the open and discussed, as well as the positive features of any deal.

d) Emotional Capital. Not only is Financial 'due diligence' practised, but also 'emotional' due diligence. This is underwritten by the belief that, whilst spreadsheets are important to financial dealings, it is people who actually make the profits and losses.

e) Profit Principles. Whilst it is essential for profits to be realised from any venture, this is not the sole criterion. 'Profit Plus' denotes their criteria and looks for long-term positive environmental and social benefits, as well as making money.

What these ladies are achieving exemplifies a new approach that introduces a new balance into the singular thinking of the past.

I also find it particularly exciting that these powerful values have now been applied to a new venture by Halla – Sisters Capital – in Copenhagen, spreading the word and the philosophy to the world.

These examples of women and their broader, new thinking are but an infinitesimal sample of what is happening across the globe and is symptomatic of the natural phenomenon of a *tipping point* referred to earlier.

> *If liberty and equality, as is thought by some, are chiefly to be found in democracy, they will be best attained when all persons alike share in government to the utmost.*
>
> ARISTOTLE

Whilst women relentlessly pursue their rightful place as equal members of *team humanity*, there is also a responsibility upon men, for all of the reasons given previously, to recognise the failings of the traditional imbalance that has existed within our species.

The *Battle of the Sexes* has been going on since we inhabited this Planet and it will continue, but hopefully in a more constructive fashion than previously. The Internet is, once again, pioneering this more balanced environment, where access is available without discrimination, as it increasingly permeates into our wider and more traditional culture.

How will the empowerment of women change us as a species? I have no idea outside of my absolute conviction that our endless conflicts with each other will subside dramatically. I am also convinced that a more caring, feminine influence will broaden our awareness and attention beyond immediate short-term goals and ambitions, something we desperately need to move away from in our present predicament.

Bringing us into greater balance as a species can only improve our overall quality of Life, by fully empowering that part of us which has been subdued for far too long. This empowerment, supported by a greater understanding of how we function, can only steer the steady Evolution of our species into a more balanced way of living Life as a Global Society.

It is a huge challenge, for both genders, in tackling an issue that is at the very core of how we function. However, I am reassured by knowing that, here, we could truly apply the wisdom of Albert Einstein in bringing new thinking to the catastrophic problems we are now facing. Whilst there are many dedicated projects worldwide furthering the development of women's place in an equal Society, there is the need for a united global impetus if we are to stand any chance of dealing effectively with our looming destruction. We have nothing to lose and absolutely everything to gain by grasping the nettle and reaping the many benefits a new and more balanced culture can provide us with, as we peer into the growing storm clouds of the future.

The character of women shaping our history across the centuries

'Hold the cross high so I may see it through the flames!'

JOAN OF ARC, 1412–1431
BEFORE BEING BURNT TO DEATH

'To have courage for whatever comes in life – everything lies in that.'

ST TERESA OF AVILA, 1515–1582

'I know I have the body of a weak and feeble woman, but I have the heart and stomach of a king.'

QUEEN ELIZABETH I, 1533–1603

'Power without a nation's confidence is nothing.'

CATHERINE THE GREAT, 1729–1796

'Finite to fail, but infinite to venture.'

EMILY DICKINSON, 1830–1886

'I can stand out the war with any man.'

FLORENCE NIGHTINGALE, 1820–1910
ABOUT THE HORRORS OF THE CRIMEAN WAR

'Nothing in life is to be feared, it is only to be understood. Now is the time to understand more, so that we may fear less.'

MARIE CURIE, 1867–1934

'We have to free half of the human race, the women, so that they can help to free the other half.'

EMMELINE PANKHURST, 1858–1928

'Those who do not move do not notice their chains.'

ROSA LUXEMBURG, 1870–1919

'We are not interested in the possibilities of defeat. They do not exist.'

QUEEN VICTORIA, 1819–1901

Our 'Mate' Planet Earth ... and the Canute Factor

Our lack of responsibility in how we treat our Planet is now reaching catastrophic proportions as we slowly poison 70% of its surface – the sea. For me, the most frightening prospect is the plastic and toxic waste we have dumped into this seemingly vast arena.

Science has discovered that this refuse is breaking down and being consumed by the smallest of sea life. This toxic waste is then passed up the food chain until, eventually, it ends up as a 'fish & chip supper' on our plates. If ever the phrase 'what goes round comes round' has credibility, it is in this cycle of poisoning, and its impact does not bear thinking about.

We have to take responsibility ... there is nobody else! JTC

When I was young, I once played the role of King Canute in a classroom production. I remember the thrill of standing up in front of the whole class and commanding the incoming tide to turn back.

For years, I thought the story of King Canute was about an egotistical sovereign falling for the fawning praise of his court, who insisted that he was all-powerful and could command the omnipotent forces of the Nature. Canute, of course, went down to the seashore with his throne and court, commanded the waves to turn back and they all got their feet wet!

As I later learnt, his were not the actions of an egotist, but someone of considerable humility, wisdom and understanding. He stood down his sycophantic courtiers by showing them that, in spite of his power, material possessions and elevated position in Society, it was Nature that was omnipotent.

To my mind, there is a logical progression from Canute to the thinking behind *Gaia* in shaping our relationship with our Planet. Professor James Lovelock's radical thinking, that this Planet is a living organism capable of looking after itself, is gradually gaining greater acceptance.

This new thinking is the crucial ammunition we need to change traditional thinking, which has created an abusive relationship with the sole provider of everything that supports our existence – *from the minute we are born to the moment we die.*

Perhaps it is this very ability to provide, seemingly without effort which has encouraged traditional thinking and beliefs to endorse our pillaging of any and all natural resources the Earth provides with a contempt impossible to quantify.

Our ingenuity is now enabling us to take from the Planet at a faster pace than it can be replaced, accelerating the looming food and water shortages we will have to face. Our financial disciplines demand we source as cheaply as possible and then sell at the highest price. It is these beliefs which are responsible for this wanton desecration of the Planet's available resources because they are *free* ... and it doesn't get much cheaper than that!

Our current relationship with our Planet is eclectic, to say the least, and reflects back at us our diverse character as a species. This is demonstrated by the manner in which we interact with our natural environment.

In the summer of 2010, we witnessed one of the greatest man-made disasters in our history, as hundreds of thousands of gallons of oil, from a ruptured drilling well, spilled into the sea in the Gulf of Mexico. Whilst there have been vast financial settlements, they must pale into insignificance when we are ultimately able to define the real toll of this tragedy.

For decades we have cleared great swathes of rainforest, our activity increasing proportionately to technological developments designed to radically bring down the time it takes to gather each hectare of timber.

In the oceans, we follow a similar pattern as we move from taking enough sea life for our daily needs to the development of *factory* ships that can stay away for months at a time. New technology snakes across the seabed, *vacuuming up* everything in its path, without distinction as to whether it is edible or not, nor the irreversible damage it is doing to our oceanic pantry.

These examples are, however, balanced to an extent, by a more positive side to our species. This is the passionate interest we exhibit across the globe to every facet of this amazing Planet we reside upon.

> *From the water, the trees, the flowers, the grass, the dirt comes life of every description ... and we respond with a microscopic curiosity of every single aspect of our Planet's activity.* JTC

This manifests in popular interest such as animal watching across every known species, and the equally committed study of all known flowers and fauna. Some passionately commit their lives to following just one species of plant or wildlife, gathering vast amounts of minute detail about their chosen subject.

I watched one person bring great intimacy to this activity by studying just a square yard of grass in his garden. He does this throughout the year and never tires of the variety of activity and wildlife constantly at work in this minute patch of our beautiful Planet.

We have people who are no less ardent in their pursuits, specialising in somewhat more obscure facets of our Planet's activity. The commitment of geyser watchers at Yellowstone National Park in America takes this interest in our Planet to a whole new level.

One woman has been watching these phenomena for over 40 years, and three people join her as wardens, cleaning the rubbish left by visitors just so they can be with these geysers as constantly as possible.

My favourite obscure pursuit is that of a man who measures the circumference of trees. In a short documentary, he trekked across vast areas of plain and hillside, wrapping a tape measure around different trunks. On one occasion, he had to hang from the side of a cliff edge whilst taking the measurement of a large trunk that was jutting out from the side of a mountain.

His passion for his subject was no less than that displayed by the infinite myriad of subjects followed by millions of enthusiasts delving into the workings of our Planet, no matter what their race, colour, gender or creed. We cannot help but be a part of this Planet because, collectively, we seek to understand everything about it. If it were not so we would ignore it ... but we can't!

> *'The earth which sustains humanity must not be injured. It must not be destroyed!'*
>
> HILDEGARDE OF BINGEN, GERMANY, 1098–1178

If these actions of interest and concern demonstrate that we are capable of treating this beautiful Planet as we do a friend, then it is not unreasonable to suggest that this global activity also demonstrates respect.

This is critically important as all relationships, no matter whether family, friendship, business or even acquaintances, are unable to function for the benefit of all concerned unless there is a quotient of respect.

> *The highest reward for a person's toil is not what they get for it, but what they become by it.*
>
> JOHN RUSKIN

It is here that we reach the *crux of the problem facing civilisation today. All too often we take others for granted and, in so doing,* abuse the most precious gifts any of us have to give during our lifetime – our time.

Our awesome Planet gives its time 24/7 in a service of total commitment to providing all we need to support our existence on Earth.

There is not a single thing we can produce, manufacture, eat or drink that is possible without the involvement of the Earth. We have lost sight of this important aspect of our lives, as we seek to produce even more materialist appendages as *consumers,* to support our seemingly fragile personal existence.

This fallibility means that, all too often, we lose sight of the contribution this totally supportive *friend* makes to our lives. This contempt with which we treat our Planet can only ever create distance between us where there should be an ever growing bond in a mutually rewarding relationship.

> *Our planet functions like any living being in optimal health – it thrives when in balance, is fuelled by the intention to always manage its balance and relies on the energy of Life itself for sustenance.* JTC

There are countless examples of our on-going mistreatment of our Planet that are witness to this contempt for its blind service to us. To get a better understanding of just how bad our abuse of our Planet has become we could take a trip in DSV Shinkai 6500, a manned research submersible run by the Japan Agency for Marine-Earth Science and Technology. This ingenious piece of equipment is capable of taking us down 18000 feet to the floor of the ocean, where we would expect to see all sorts of incredible deep sea life rarely, if at all seen before this craft was invented. Instead of sea life what is presented to us is the results of countless years of irresponsible abuse with a sea floor littered with our waste, from plastic bags and bottles, to even a broken toy doll according to one report … and that was over 20 years ago. What must our vast chosen *Rubbish Tip* look like now?!

Would we think of dropping this unwanted litter on our friend's carpet or garden lawn? I don't think so – it would not even enter our heads. However, the size and silence of our Planet means we find it unnecessary to question its supposed unstinting ability to clear up after us, as a parent might after a small, recalcitrant child.

> *The Plastiki Voyage was conceived by Team Earth in 2010 to draw attention to a vast garbage patch floating in the Pacific Ocean. How vast – twice the size of Texas! This illustrates our need to understand better how to manage and dispose of the 'continents' of plastic we manufacture each year.* JTC

I bring this element of judgement in here, not as criticism but to emphasise how our thinking and belief create the world we live in. We have never considered the Planet to be *our Mate* and this is reflected in how we treat it, something that is now coming back to bite us – and bite us ever harder!

When you add to this the devastation caused by modern fishing technology, which was touched upon earlier, and a Planet that comprises 70% of sea, we appear to be playing Russian roulette with our own survival. We are polluting our own food … what other species on Earth does this?

Within this chapter about Planet Earth, I have deliberately stayed away from the subject of climate change. It currently stands firmly in the courts of vested interest, battling for dominance of their respective view of the problem, rather than reaching to the cause, as I see it.

However, the growing numbers of natural and devastating catastrophes now occurring, whether from climate change or not, highlight the limitations in our traditional thinking. These limitations, in turn, also limit the relationship we have with our *Mate-in-waiting.*

What I found particularly scary was a simple story that makes clear how dangerous the balance now is. We know that the Earth's crust is relatively thin and that melting polar caps are redistributing vast tonnages of water around the globe, as evidenced by rising water levels. This redistribution must have an impact upon this thin surface layer of the Planet *because of the sheer weight of the volumes of water involved.*

Could this be why we are now experiencing so many volcanoes and other sizeable eruptions, as our Planet shifts its tectonic plates in response to these new pressures – as we might when shifting a heavy suitcase from our hand to our shoulder?

Instead of placing it *front and centre* as a priority task to better understand and do something about it, we get angry because these natural disasters have an adverse effect upon our financial bottom line.

In a strong relationship, we recognise and try to understand and accept each other's strengths and weaknesses. Surely, in our relationship with our Planet, in return for providing us with all we need, it is not unreasonable to be more understanding of its own idiosyncrasies and their impact upon our activities.

> ***Financial Statistics and Nature***
>
> *An ongoing project known as The Economics of Ecosystems and Biodiversity has calculated the loss of forests alone at $2–5 trillion a year, given the contribution they make to clean water supply and absorbing carbon dioxide, numbers that dwarf the costs of the banking crisis.* JTC

Its elevation to greater prominence as *our Mate* might accelerate the change in our attitude, by promoting a stronger desire to become better acquainted with our newfound friend. As with any new friend, our first objective is to better understand them and find out what makes them tick.

By changing the way we think about our relationship with Planet Earth, we can approach many of the critical problems we are currently facing from a whole new direction. This is yet another perfect example of how we function as Creators, sowing new seeds in our minds that obsolete old beliefs and then change our circumstances.

Leadership that carries the wisdom of *the Canute factor* would recognise that we are not above the forces of this Planet, but very much subject to them, and need to adapt our behaviour accordingly.

Never has this been truer than in the financial abyss we now face. We became detached from *our Mate* when we gave greater importance to the value of our money.

There is a part of me that can see how the gold standard we used to value our paper money was also a means by which our Planet *subliminally* regulated our use of money, like any true friend. As I have said previously, since we stopped using this natural resource to manage our use of money its value has inflated, whilst the natural resources we buy continue to remain unchanged.

I believe our Planet looks after us, and all other species, in ways like this that we have never considered before, and we need to recognise and find a new respect for our relationship with *our Mate.*

Building this respect would manifest a myriad of opportunities for us in creating new jobs and industries, supporting our proper role as *Stewards* of this Planet. It would also further unite us as a species with this shared responsibility towards our *common* Mate.

> ***Kestrel Consciousness***
>
> *I was walking a range of hills when I noticed a Kestrel hovering as it searched for its next meal. I was above it on a hill and, in spite of a strong wind that nearly took my cap off, I was able to line this amazing creature up with the landscape of an adjacent hill. It was totally at one with its environment, simply moving its wings and tail feathers whilst keeping its head motionless as it searched for prey below. That is the target for humanity … Kestrel Consciousness – to become at one with our planetary environment.* JTC

The Birthing of a Global Society

At the dawning of this 21st century, the massive increase in human migration is resulting in a growing diversity within the populations of nearly every country in the world, and a subsequent confusion over national values. Tension is further exacerbated where migrants are not accepted in their countries of final destination. The speed in growth of this 'melting pot' of people, with differing values and ideals, is contributing to the lack of understanding and intolerance in what has now become the infant Global Village. The needs of the corporate world have fuelled global migration, and the growing pains we are now experiencing come from our inability to fully understand the vast implications of our narrowly defined actions. This confusion is further evidence of human Evolution at work, and the challenge today is to recognise this and take charge of our destiny, rather than continue as its slave. JTC

Our newfound ability to communicate directly with each other, and more easily travel anywhere around the globe, is leading to a greater understanding of the unity of Life on Planet Earth.

For human beings, there is nothing more effective than experiencing something directly. It has been proven over time to always dispel ignorance and stimulate positive thinking and interaction, as illustrated earlier in our experience with whales.

This is some comfort, given the many very real challenges that confront us now, as Evolution pushes us together with ever greater velocity into a new Global Society.

The advent of the Internet means that the traditional dynamics by which we have previously interacted as a species have changed forever.

For people like me, who were born after the last World War, we grew up within traditional beliefs about race, colour, gender and creed that have not only separated us as a species but could also separate us from neighbours, friends and even family.

These beliefs created barriers of ignorance between us and these supposed *foreigners*, further aggravated by our restricted ability to travel, meet and get to know these *strangers* in other parts of the world. Our perceptions and beliefs about each other were shaped by what we were told.

The greatest friend of truth is Time, her greatest enemy is Prejudice, and her constant companion is Humility.

CHARLES CALEB COLTON

Whilst increasing immigration began to bring us together, within these growing communities of differing colours and creeds, the traditional *barriers* of belief continued to cause tension and conflict. Often, rather than become an outsider in our own community, we bent to popular consensus and adopted the *uniform* of racism, helping maintain and continue Society's barriers of separation.

In Britain and America, there has been a gradual but painful erosion of these barriers as vast influxes of immigrants from across the globe have changed the social landscape. Even after two centuries, however, tensions still erupt in America, which have been mirrored after only a few decades of immigration in Britain and other European countries.

If we project forward just a few decades into the 21st century, the non-white population will constitute a majority of the citizens in the US. Reports suggest that many white evangelical Christians feel besieged by immigrants or minorities who appear to be *taking over.*

At the heart of this current fear might be the realisation that the *suppressors* could become the *suppressed,* if we continue to allow these *uniforms* any credibility. Those who fear may do so because they remember the actions of their forebears just two centuries earlier towards the Native Americans, and the gradual suppression of that proud nation's way of Life.

The glowing embers of these tensions are now being fanned in an infant Global Village, where the pace of migration is dramatically accelerating. With a growing awareness of what is going on beyond their traditional homelands, families are seeking a better Life elsewhere. Business and governments, too, are seeking young labour that is cheap to employ, and who will also support the financing of a growing retirement population.

Whilst it is the responsibility of every family to seek the best Life it can, surely there is also a need to expand this responsibility by also *respecting* the new values of the countries of their chosen destination.

In the West, we recognise and have grown up with *freedom of speech,* for example. Here, we see it not only as a human right, but also as a strength in highlighting potential flaws in Society, using it to change current perspectives and beliefs. We recognise that it is by this very freedom that we build confidence and unity in the community, something not easily recognised by those escaping harsh and restrictive environments elsewhere.

We have seen resentment at perceived criticisms by those not brought up in a healthy environment of free speech, which can then turn to anger and a desire to repress this freedom. This action, if successful, would lead Society into the type of repressive regime many of these immigrants have left behind. As a species, we are not capable of returning to the negative experiences of the past, and so here we have a new opportunity to direct the future course of our collective destinies.

If we collectively choose not to repress Society, but rather to gain the confidence of new members, through proper education and time, we are managing this aspect of our Evolution *in a tried and tested tango of 3 forward and 2 back.*

Surely, this is at the very heart of global integration as we constantly seek to learn from each other, recognising and adopting the strengths that can unite us, whilst dropping the weaknesses which keep us apart.

Another aspect of the struggle facing migrants comes from a political and corporate environment where the needs of one faction of Society are met at the cost to other factions. In the UK, financial considerations are becoming a growing cause of social unrest, as monetary support is provided to new immigrants who have obviously not previously contributed to the *communal* pot, thus reducing the overall quality of Life for those who have.

It is here that we reach the very heart of the problems our traditional belief systems now present us with in restricting the nurturing of a Global Society.

The development of multiculturalism to meet financial criteria in the corporate world, supported by traditional religious and political beliefs that have kept us separated as a species, is producing a growing friction where we should be seeking unity. Little attention is given to the fundamentals of what separates us and, until we confront this issue, we will have an environment in which terrorism can ferment with ease.

It is another task of monumental proportions that lies ahead, not only for our traditional institutions, but also for every man, woman and child. Hearts and minds have to move away from the separatist traditional thinking and teachings that have ruled our lives for generations, if we are truly to become a Global Village.

It will become essential for all of us to reach out to each other, if we are to end the constant conflicts of the past; to recognise that we are one species ... and we are all dealing with similar problems and *goals.*

It is not unlike moulding a national football team, whose members are drawn from different clubs, all of whom are talented players. It is the task of the manager to get these players to interact as a team, supporting each other with their individual strengths and abilities. It takes time, but a growing familiarity between the members and their talents breeds acceptance and trust, as well as a respect for what each member has to offer – critical ingredients in welding together a well-functioning and motivated team.

Recognising this challenge is perhaps the biggest hurdle we currently face, if we are to move forward with the minimum of historic conflict. Having truly recognised this, however, it all gets a lot easier with the next step, which is creative thinking to resolve the problem ... something, fortunately, we excel at!

Already, in our journey towards a Global Society, there are signs of evolutionary change, as the young are showing themselves to be the greatest harbingers of racial cohesion through another of Life's endless paradoxes.

Whilst their parents struggle with beliefs they have held all of their lives in a Society that is rapidly changing, their children only know the structure of a multicultural society. They are, to an extent, free of the prejudices of their parents and grandparents, united in classrooms where they can recognise the same characteristics inherent in children the world over, namely their passion for *footballs, dolls, clothes and iPods.*

The Internet has provided them with the means to create the face of an emerging Global Society of '*Facebookers*' and '*YouTubers*'. This new Society that comprises Muslims, Catholics, Satanists, Mechanics, Lawyers, Black, White, Brown, Male and Female, is already driving a coach and horses through the traditionally separatist barriers of thinking and belief.

When you consider that, it was postulated there were more people connected by Facebook in 2012 than *lived* on this beautiful Planet 200 years ago, we are able to recognise just how radically, and irreversibly, this Evolutionary development has changed in how we interact as a species.

Groups of *like-minded people* are forming under new banners that further break down the old and somewhat controlling order, introducing a freer and more *organic* process of social integration. They are increasingly working together to solve the problems they identify – both their own and those of others.

> *Like the grains of sand that make a beach, unity is not about being the same, but bringing together the myriad of different people and cultures to reveal the wonder of our species.* JTC

As traditional perspectives enter the arena of a global audience, even beliefs that were previously branded as *occult* are finding a new voice and social respect. The new freedom of the Internet is gradually removing any tarnish from these beliefs that may have accumulated over the centuries from vested interests.

Our evolving Society is now able to access vast amounts of data about our history as a species. This is liberating people everywhere to make their own informed choices about the values they place upon the Life they seek to create for themselves, something which, again, was previously influenced by our traditional institutions.

The Internet has become the primary unifying force behind Globalisation because it is able to mimic the basic functioning of all Life on this Planet. Like a plant, animal or human being, the Internet is a conglomeration of individual cells (users) working in unison to make it function and evolve.

It is the *heart* of our newly-emerging Global Society, carefully mirroring how we function as human beings and pulsating to our collective activity. From the blogs of individuals read by a few, to the viral activity of authors and others whose work and views touch a collective artery, it is stimulating a new unity we have never recognised, nor been capable of before.

The power of this unifying force is causing new values to emerge from a more informed majority, as Evolution pushes Society to replace outmoded traditional thinking. Indeed, it is difficult to see how the old thinking can be sustained, as it becomes clearer that it simply no longer addresses or aligns with the new reality we are creating.

We will have to live in a more tolerant world where differing religious beliefs are recognised and accepted as the means of nourishing our spiritual needs, rather than the tool for seeking domination through conflict.

After millennia of maligning each other, the task ahead for all religious institutions, and particularly those already suffering credibility issues, will be immense. However, I believe that the seeds of their salvation and rebirth lie within this daunting task.

Political decision-making will have to become more transparent in order to demonstrate to the growing multicultural societies in all countries that governments are seeking to unite and benefit them globally.

For this transparency to regain the support of the majority, it will need to be seen to recognise and accept that we all face the same challenges in this 21st century and it is time to replace our *uniforms* with humanity's *overalls*.

It will, therefore, become increasingly difficult for those in government to ignore this collective activity as our new communications systems continue to highlight the common themes of the many *global* protests seeking greater balance between our Planet and its inhabitants. The rise in support for the *Occupy Movement,* which began in Wall Street, has rapidly hit a tipping point and mushroomed across the oceans to Europe and Asia.

The nature of this support is evidence of the foundations being laid for a global democracy that is linked by ideology and belief, something that was previously the province of religion and politics, as the Internet increasingly reflects the views of the many in mirroring all that we do.

This new democracy, which I can see being driven by Charitable endeavour will, I suspect, not be managed by a *top-down* hierarchy, but reflect the collective ethos of a growing like-minded Global Society who seek to balance the needs of our business communities with those of this Planet and its inhabitants.

They can only achieve this by supporting politicians and governments with a similar mind-set, whose transparency is evidenced by their achievements in meeting the wishes of the majority. There will also be a desire to preserve National identities as countries seek to work together *within a collective global consensus proposed and supported by the people.*

I fervently believe that the new Global Village and its Society can only function successfully by continuing to recognise and respect national identities and our diversity as a species. In so doing, we recognise, respect and follow the natural order that is inherent in all aspects of Life.

My perception of the European Union is that it has been created and driven by political belief alone and that, in consequence, the democratic process became lost over the years in the expanding bureaucracy.

Indeed, the whole structure of the EU is now under discussion as nation states within the Union are seeking repatriation of powers given over previously. In the case of crime, for example, individual states know they can work more efficiently together without the need for central police forces and courts of law.

This is an important lesson in government. The greater the consolidation of power, the less efficient the democratic process becomes as the vested interests of the few takes precedent over the many. From the experience of the EU, the concept of a global government would be unlikely to get out of the starting gate.

> *A government is like fire, a handy servant, but a dangerous master.*
>
> GEORGE WASHINGTON

I cannot emphasise enough this need for us to mirror how the Natural world functions. The greater the variety of contribution and support, the more balanced our environment, as it reflects the diverse needs of the whole.

I believe that another powerful driving force in our unification as a species, in addition to the Internet, global travel and communications technology, will be the desire to resolve the problems of growing food, water and other Planetary resource shortages, that have been created by our traditional thinking.

If we choose to take it, our journey into a Global Society will propel us to seek out new solutions that will better manage human fallibility as we go about tackling the problems we now face. By understanding and accepting more fully how we function, we can look forward to taking far greater control over our destiny and managing our future Evolutionary progress together.

PART 3: FROM MAGNA CARTA TO GLOBAL MAGNA CARTA

The Case for a Global Magna Carta

We shall require a substantially new manner of thinking if humanity is to survive.

(My interpretation again of more great wisdom from Albert Einstein)

The continuous abuses of the majority by a king who thought he was above the law led to the creation of Magna Carta in 1215, effectively ending that abuse by containing his powers. Eight hundred years later, we are again witness to similar abuses of the majority. The threats this time around, however, are not just restricted to one country and its population, but are of global proportions because of our current stage of Evolution as a species.

I have carried the message throughout this book that we create Life on Planet Earth through what we think and come to believe in. When the beliefs we create are subsequently found not to work in our long-term interests, or we outgrow them, new thinking evolves.

This happens because the old thinking is incapable of resolving the problems it created and eventually becomes obsolete. We then continue our journey in another direction with new thinking that can sometimes also see us repeating the mistakes of the past.

Traditionally, this simple but omnipotent process has only ever caused us to react to change through fear, resulting in a never-ending cycle of conflict as the old thinking resists the new and the change it is creating. The time has now arrived, I believe, for another 'Magna Carta Moment' where, once again, we confront and change our current thinking and beliefs.

Profiting from growing food and water shortages, and fighting amongst ourselves over those same diminishing resources, can only ever result in our nuclear destruction. We are now so preoccupied with enslavement to debt and imprisonment by terrorism that it is causing us to lose sight of the ONLY problem we should now be addressing, that of our future survival. (Once we have resolved this problem, we can go back to debt and terrorism if we feel so moved.)

Collectively, we – the 1% and the 99% – are responsible. *The buck stops with us and no one else.* How we halt this particular tide can only come from new thinking and values that better support the management of our Planetary resources and encourage the unity of our species at this critical time, as well as into the future.

You never change things by fighting the existing reality. To change something, build a new model that makes the existing model obsolete.

RICHARD BUCKMINSTER FULLER

To do this, we need to look at *watering down the intensity of our current beliefs* by broadening their application to Life. By moving 180 degrees from our present narrow financial thinking, we place ourselves in a more positive and nurturing environment that is more conducive to how we function.

This environment of preservation, compassion and long-term broader thinking has always been the cornerstone of our global charitable activities. Here, we find unifying disciplines that motivate the desire to improve our quality of Life across the complete spectrum of human activity, from Humanity to Nature and every other facet of Life on this beautiful Planet.

Just consider the power of the words we use to identify the institutions we have created: Friends of the Earth, Amnesty International, Greenpeace and so on. These titles are witness to a mind-set and attitude that is quite the reverse of that driving our current financial disciplines and practices.

It is within this environment that we find the abdication of gender dominance, and a financial and political arena, that is focussed upon *supporting* our endeavours, rather than being the *goal* of those endeavours. By turning towards broader, life-sustaining thinking and beliefs, I would suggest that we align more closely with what we are all about and move positively to becoming *Mastresses* (Mistresses and Masters) of our future Evolution.

The positive effects of this simple change to our dominant thinking becomes quite staggering if we look more closely at just two aspects – the role women play in this thing called Life and our attitude to food production.

> *We revere Profit and strip our Planet, instead of the other way around.* JTC

Our dominant religious beliefs have, for millennia, dictated our attitude to the role of women in Society, limiting the contribution they make to the healthy and balanced Evolution of our species.

If our dominant belief were Wicca, we would see women with an equal status to their male counterparts and making an equal contribution to running Society. (These same beliefs also demand that they are regularly updated to reflect the current manner in which we live Life.)

Let me take the whole subject of equal status for women one step further, as it is a subject I am passionate about! The horrendous conflicts occurring across our Planet are witness to a new terror as rape is applied increasingly as a strategic military action.

In 2013, the conflict in Syria has seen the use of chemical weapons triggering the international community to become involved as the situation continues to deteriorate.

Suppose instead of, or in addition to, chemical weapons, *rape* was the crime that triggered that same international community into action. How much would that rein in the escalating humanitarian abuses we now perpetrate within modern warfare? How much would it elevate the respect and status of women across the world *and our overall game as a species?*

When we turn our attention elsewhere, surely the need to recognise and commit to the maintenance and support of our *collective* home – Planet Earth – and all it provides us with must come at the top of our list of necessary changes. With this simple commitment comes a vast ripple effect in engendering a global unification of purpose that touches every single one of us, irrespective of race, colour, creed and gender.

Applying this new attitude to our food, for example, means it will no longer be traded on markets solely for financial gain, causing hardship for the poor when intense market activity forces prices to escalate. Our food production will also undergo change, no longer being driven by the quest for profit that places at risk its nutritional content and the subsequent threat to our long-term health and welfare.

(This last point must become more pertinent to future thinking about our health and wellbeing, given the World Health Organisation's concerns that our bodies are now becoming increasingly immune to the use of antibiotics. Maximising the nutritional content of our food becomes a priority if we do not want to see a return to the Dark Ages, where a simple scratch could become life-threatening.)

By recognising the need to maximise the nutritional quality of our food, we add impetus to the wider issues on how we effectively manage our Planet's resources, adding another ingredient to the unification of purpose we now need across global politics.

By simply changing current dominating beliefs from Capitalism driven by Profitable endeavour to Capitalism driven by Charitable endeavour, this new mind-set would look to the repair and maintenance of our Planet, rather than its blind destruction. In this manner, we subtly change our thinking from profit-driven *consumption* to profit-driven *sustenance*. Be under no illusion, however – there is profit to be made for sustaining our environment.

(It is not the province of this book to judge the merits or otherwise of factory farming, nor individual belief systems, but simply to demonstrate that the manner in which we live our lives is directly reflected by our dominant beliefs.)

It is here, with a growing global momentum supporting this thinking, that I see the birthing of a new *Middle Way* political party. This political party would have a global understanding and commitment that offers an alternative to the traditional political doctrines of Left and Right, perpetually aligned to the demands of the relevant vested interests.

> *When the habitually even-tempered suddenly fly into a passion, that explosion is apt to be more impressive than the outburst of the most violent amongst us.*
>
> MARGERY ALLINGHAM

This *Middle Way* can only evolve from the charitable sector within Society, in my opinion, and would be at the heart of the new dominant thinking we need to adopt for our future survival. I say this because the people and services involved represent one of the few sectors that now hold Society's trust and respect, through their nurturing and transparent ethos towards this Planet and its inhabitants.

Certainly, there are millions of people across the globe with the charitable mind-set necessary to drive the change we now need, and a sufficient pool from which to elect a new breed of politicians into the democratic process. They would be easily identified by their commitment to implement the Core Beliefs of a Global Magna Carta that returns power to the 99% and births a New Democracy.

What a sea change it would encourage within our present political environment as current, short-term thinking is replaced by an agenda that plans for decades ahead. The short-term needs of the party would be replaced by the long-term needs of the Planet and its Inhabitants. Within this new environment, traditional beliefs that are leading to our destruction would become obsolete.

Where once we donated voluntarily to people we trusted to spend our money responsibly on causes we believed in, we would now hand our money over in the form of taxes to those we have elected to manage Society. We would do in the certain knowledge that it will be used responsibly to manage our interactions with this beautiful Planet and each other. What a change this would make in our attitude towards paying taxes.

I believe the ground is already being prepared for this change as the Evolutionary process begins to destabilise the present status quo. I see this reflected in disruptive thinking behind expanding forms of state abuse that are building growing Social unrest. The transparency now provided by the Internet is encouraging ever-growing whistle-blower activity as people react to abuses, both old and new.

It is also evident in the actions of such business icons as Bill Gates, who has been reported to have committed to giving away 95% of his wealth before he dies. This truly is the flagship of this new environment of charitable profit, where the money follows the Natural cycle in being returned to its fundamental source of origin.

As this protest expands, the credibility of our institutions is now being taken to a tipping point beyond which they will struggle to retain the support of those who have been so systematically abused. Indeed, intense reaction by governments to whistle-blower activity, such as WikiLeaks, Chelsea Manning and Edward Snowden, is returning America to the horrors of the McCarthy era as millions of federal workers in the intelligence community are being pressured into spying upon each other.

Such extreme actions can only ever stimulate increasingly more extreme *reactions,* sending us towards George Orwell's 1984 as human nature, at its most basic, enters the perpetual spiral of recrimination.

As the credibility of current beliefs evaporates at an accelerating pace, those seeking to hold onto power incite further protest by their every action. From violent repression to mass surveillance, the compulsive desire to retain power is now moving into self-destruct mode and causing a sea-change across Society at large and the young in particular.

> ***Integrity is manifesting through the young***
>
> *When 29-year-old US analyst, Edward Snowden, declared he was the source of the Guardian newspaper's exposure on the increased US surveillance of Internet users, he made it quite clear that he did not seek to 'hide from justice, but reveal criminality'. 'I don't want to live in a world where there's no privacy and therefore no room for intellectual exploration and creativity.'*
>
> *Among the many reactions to his disclosures from Internet users, something that encapsulated popular sentiment for me was a cartoon showing a dinosaur in the background and a government quoted sentiment 'If you're not doing anything wrong, you shouldn't have anything to hide.' Beneath this, the response read 'If that is true, shouldn't the government declassify everything?'*
>
> *I see Evolution at work here, wielding the powerful forces of Integrity by demanding greater oversight, transparency and accountability from our governments. In an age where the vast majority of contractors employed by security services are intelligent young people like Snowden, I would think it almost impossible to contain his brand of integrity.* JTC

Indebted students have paid much financially for their education, but are also now sufficiently educated to understand the plight we all face.

They see a personal future environment where they are unable to gain employment and provide a home in which to raise a family, depriving them of the experience of the most basic of human functions, added to which their every move is being recorded.

They recognise that traditional beliefs will escalate the price of food and water when shortages begin to bite, whilst remaining incapable of resolving the problem. The Internet is telling them of hedge funds increasingly becoming involved and making money from shortages in commodity supplies, as well as making substantial investments in farms and all manner of food production for future profit.

They also recognise that the only outcome from flawed beliefs now shaping their lives is a Planet that could be covered in nuclear waste during their lifetime. It will be them that *peacefully* rise up against growing totalitarian oppression.

I am sure they now seek a new environment in which *all* compromise, power and financial implication can only ever be for the *benefit* of this beautiful Planet and its wonderful inhabitants, *created by new dominant beliefs.*

Within a growing environment that is driven by the ethos of the charitable sector, Society can only ever be directed towards a more *collectively* managed future. Here, we can confidently and transparently address the looming food and water shortages *and win*, supported by beliefs that begin to address and remedy our abuses of the past.

This new thinking in no way invalidates many of the traditional party and corporate doctrines, because Life would not be possible without them. Indeed, it is only those charities with sound financial and business disciplines that survive and expand.

The biggest demand for change would come for the Left and Right to adapt and unite, as both employers and employees accept a common agenda that is dictated by the real challenges we are all soon to face.

Our corporate and social activities would reflect the priorities of a new unifying ethos, where profit has become just one of several criteria that would direct how we come together as a species and better manage our Planet.

If we now draw breath for a moment, I hope I have clearly demonstrated how our thinking would create a new reality by changing from Capitalism driven by Profitable endeavour to Capitalism driven by Charitable endeavour. Utilising our established democratic process, the emphasis shifts towards those representatives we have elected, whose new (longer-term) thinking will meet the broader spectrum of human and planetary demands capable of addressing our dwindling global resources.

> *On a visit to Highgrove, the home of His Royal Highness The Prince of Wales for over 30 years now, I was moved by the story of the sheer magnificence of the 200 year old Cedar of Lebanon tree by the main house that decided The Prince to buy the property. Sadly the tree became diseased and had to be felled in 2007. In its place The Prince had an oak pavilion with church like spire constructed with a small oak tree by its side. The reasoning I was told was that by the time the spire rotted down there would be a fully mature oak tree to replace the Cedar of Lebanon that he had been so fond of.*

On a similar visit to Blenheim Palace, I was in awe of the gardens and grounds in which the beautiful buildings resided. They had been designed by the gardening genius 'Capability' Brown. It was then that I realised that this incredible man worked all of his life on projects, the true beauty of which he, like The Prince of Wales, would never live to see in their full glory. We desperately need leaders now with this commitment and nurturing foresight. JTC

In confronting and changing the thinking and reactions of millennia, it is essential that we recognise and accept WITHOUT JUDGEMENT that any and all abuse comes from human fallibility, and is something we are *all* capable of. By taking this first faltering, but massive, step, we can begin the change towards a better management and regulation of our extreme behaviour through a more unified and involved Society.

Only by our collective understanding and support can the Evolutionary process be recognised for the contribution it makes to Life and accepted as such. With this new understanding, we are able to then introduce new beliefs and values that are more in keeping with our present stage of development as a species, changing forever how we live Life on Planet Earth. *(Remember the Stone Age – we didn't run out of stones, we outgrew them.)*

A vibrant new democracy is something far more achievable now than ever before, as improving communications tear down traditional veils of secrecy. Be under no illusion, however, as to the awesome responsibility this change will demand of our Society which, in the past, has gone along with a weak democratic process, *where it gave its power away with little or no supervision*, to an elected minority to manage.

If the people we elect do not serve the best interests of Society, then we have the ability to replace them by electing new people. True democracy can only ever work when electors recognise they have the ultimate power. There is no place for voter apathy when the 99% recognise and use this power. It was President Eisenhower who observed how bad officials were elected by good voters who didn't vote. JTC

If we accept this responsibility, it then becomes a collective commitment to ensure we never return to the traditional apathy of the past, by recognising that new thinking about a world *beyond our lifetimes* is the key to our becoming *Mastresses* of our future Evolution as a species.

Be assured that the world of Global Magna Carta is already underway in Iceland, as the following story illustrates.

Iceland, like many other countries across the globe, was brought to its knees by financial and political activity that lacked any form of transparency or accountability because of a woefully inadequate democratic system.

In February 2009, The Social Democratic-Green coalition government, led by Johanna Siguroardottir, a lady determined to introduce constitutional reform, sought to re-write the country's Constitution in spite of equally determined hostility to change from both the Supreme Court and Parliament.

Her real problem, however, was not so much the hostility but the lack of credibility in which Parliament was held by the people after all they had experienced over the past two years.

In spite of this, one determined lady and her coalition government set about repairing the damage her country had sustained by passing the historically unique Act on a Constitutional Assembly in June 2010. THIS ACT WAS UNIQUE BECAUSE IT PASSED THE TASK OF WRITING SUCH AN IMPORTANT DOCUMENT TO A GROUP OF CITIZENS, YET TO BE SELECTED, WHO WOULD RECEIVE FULL AND PROPER LEGAL SUPPORT.

The process began with a meeting of 1,500 randomly selected citizens to establish a values framework with which the document should be constructed. Once accomplished, a self-governing council was finally formed (after overcoming more hostility from opposition parties), to begin work on the construction of the new Constitution – to be presented within four months.

At all times, the Icelanders were fully involved in this process by means of television, websites and social networking sites, and their comments and suggestions were considered and debated. As this whole process was independent from political or corporate lobbying, and supported by modern communication technology, it could accurately reflect the thinking of the people in a 'live' environment between the Council and the public.

This structure was also probably responsible for the draft Constitution being submitted to Parliament within the allotted timescale, and subsequently put to the people in a referendum. This historic document is now the force that has rendered the Icelandic Parliament transparent in their dealings and accountability to the people.

This ground breaking process has also established beyond doubt the capacity of the people to collectively create a document of substance that determines the manner in which they wish to be governed – something previously held in doubt by traditional thinking.

(I am in debt to Richard Bater and his excellent thesis 'Manufacturing Transparency: composing law in an island laboratory' for drawing my attention to this incredible story.)

If thinking has to change, then I would offer Global Magna Carta as a starting point. The number of like-minded people this thinking identifies with, and who wish to become part of the change it advocates, will dictate whether this is the way forward or not. I have no preconceived ideas as to where this will take us, as my intention is to hand it over to the majority to shape and build. I am merely a catalyst.

I cannot emphasise enough that nothing is set in tablets of stone. It is for the majority to develop their campaigns around whatever Core Beliefs are collectively agreed and defined within Global Magna Carta, utilising the democratic process to take these beliefs into the mainstream to create the change they believe in.

> *Never doubt that a small group of thoughtful, committed citizens can change the world. Indeed, it is the only thing that ever has.*
>
> MARGARET MEAD

I cannot see that any change is possible without the commitment of the majority of the 99% and the acceptance of the 1%. In this way, we recognise and accept the Evolutionary process that is now taking place and, for the first time in our history, begin to manage it, rather than repeating the human misery of the past by fighting it. Apathy is no longer an option, as it is only through collective thinking that a new direction can be created, defined and taken.

Managing our Evolution by better managing our fallibilities through a new discipline, as ventured by Global Magna Carta, is my most fervent wish now. The *ending* prophesied in the Mayan Calendar stimulated my writing this book, as I can clearly see its fulfilment through one of the following two options:

1. The destruction of our species from current traditional beliefs.
2. We will see the replacement of those beliefs through the emergence of a new consensus, created by new beliefs in how we interact with each other and this beautiful Planet.

What will be the eventual outcome, either in 50 years with existing beliefs, or 250 years with increasingly sustaining new beliefs, is anyone's guess.

What is non-negotiable, however, is that the choice of ending is collectively ours ... *and ours alone.*

Global Magna Carta – A New Mind-Set

A Document of Understanding and Change, designed to encourage our Global Society into a new Relationship with itself and Planet Earth, by restoring Integrity and Mutual Respect.

General Consensus

Global Magna Carta is not designed to conflict or compete with the constitutions we have already evolved and work with, but as a catalyst for people across the whole Social spectrum to change their thinking ... if they want to.

It seeks to offer an initial infrastructure of beliefs which will support our Global Society in managing the changes that occur as a result of our ongoing Evolutionary progress. By utilising our judgement as to what works and does not work for our benefit, we can pursue the attainment of listed current goals, as directed by its Core Beliefs, driven by the spirit of the original Magna Carta.

This new mind-set recognises that all human beings are a single species, who create Life on Planet Earth by what they think and come to believe in, irrespective of gender, race, colour or creed. It is accepted that our Evolution runs in cycles of change, and resistance to this change can only ever result in painful conflict, simply delaying the inevitable new cycle we are moving towards.

Therefore, each Core Belief recognises our need as a species to constantly strive for new areas of attainment and experience in all we do, as a part of our primary driving force, which is the Evolutionary process.

It is also recognised that, within all human striving, there is human fallibility. Paramount to the spirit of these Core Beliefs is the desire to sympathetically and respectfully manage this aspect of the human condition.

Whilst it is the intention of this document to remain flexible in its content to reflect our personal development as a species, the purpose of these Core Beliefs is to maintain our respect for each other and our relationship with our Planet at all times.

Fundamental to this new mind-set is the understanding of the need for a global consensus by which we direct the management of our Evolution as a species.

Core Beliefs

1. That humanity is a single species, whose unity is paramount to our future survival. Within this understanding, there is unconditional support for any and all beliefs that seek to unite individuality within our species and, particularly, the unity of races, colours, creeds and gender.

The Evolution of an expanding Global Society is fuelling the replacement of traditional beliefs that previously supported our separation by race, colour, creed and gender. Only by collective thinking, belief and action that support the unification of our one species and its differing aspects can we positively manage our current and future Evolution. Recognising and promoting our commonality as a single species of Creators of Life on Planet Earth will reflect our new management powers in action. Working with Evolution in this fashion will manifest our basic desire to live in harmony, recognising our unity as a species, whilst respecting our differences within that unity. This will achieve our current Evolutionary goal of a Global Family, with all of the attributes of union and conflict that are prevalent in any healthy family environment.

2. The Internet is an integral part of our future unity and development as a species. Any and all regulation of its democracy will respect the maintenance of its independence, transparency and integrity.

This technology is the cornerstone of our present Evolutionary phase in uniting us as a species, pioneering new interactions across all levels of human activity. A new global democracy is being born, supporting and encouraging transparency in our dealings with each other that mirrors our highest values in how we function as a species. It is incumbent upon all of us to grow with this technology, supporting its development and learning, and adapting to any beneficial new thinking and democratic disciplines it influences. It is recognised, therefore, that its control, beyond that which is socially and morally acceptable, is in no way conducive to our future development.

3. In recognising that trade is a fundamental aspect of our species, its future development and regulation must always be governed by the need for money, or any other derivative, to never again be invested with the power to enslave humanity, both of those who have it and those who do not. To this end it is accepted that we must move from beliefs of Capitalism driven by Profitable endeavour to Capitalism driven by Charitable endeavour.

Money – As our primary tool of for trading, it is essential we manage our relationship with it in such a way as to ensure its task as a servant in uniting us, rather than dividing us as a master. Conventional wisdom dictates that monopolies in any arena of Life do not benefit the majority and, therefore, the new and diverse opportunities within our present phase of Evolution which are being presented, and might further evolve our monetary systems should be fully investigated as to their ability to serve us into the future.

Credit – Recognising and accepting that aspects of this type of financial arrangement are prone to working against the human condition, it is essential that we implement safeguards to protect human fallibility and guard against the excesses of the last two decades of the 20th century.

Capitalism – This belief system suits us well as a species of Creators. However, like all belief systems, it can present risks to Society when extreme views and activity become dominant. Whilst our ingenuity across all aspects of Life must be encouraged, it is essential that its application cannot affect those areas of Life that are essential to providing and supporting our food, clothing and shelter. Ring-fencing our activity in this manner enables us to satisfy our inherent need to push the boundaries by constantly evolving these disciplines, without threatening our very existence when mistakes occur through human fallibility. It is accepted that growth is an inherent part of ALL aspects of Life and we can, therefore, no longer restrict our belief in Capitalism to solely growth in profit without the subsequent growth in the development, support and maintenance of all the human and Planetary resources needed for its healthy maintenance. This Core Belief supports a move of emphasis therefore, from Capitalism driven by Profitable endeavour to Capitalism driven by Charitable endeavour.

4. The recognition of the need for humanity to come into balance as species, for our future peaceful coexistence and survival. This can only be achieved with the full empowerment of women, to enjoy the equal status, influence and contribution to Society that has previously been exercised by the male of the species.

The current imbalance in our male-dominated Society has been one of the main factors responsible for our circle of endless conflict with each other throughout the millennia. It is only possible to break this circle, which has constantly restricted our development as a species, by empowering women to equally influence the management of this thing called Life. Their greater ability to restrict conflict and short-term thinking, as well as their many other inherent skills, are integral to dealing with the challenges we now face.

5. By recognising the limitless ingenuity of our species, there is also the recognition and acceptance of human fallibility as an integral part of the human condition. It is seen as paramount to support and implement a Democratic process with which to effectively manage this condition with compassion, integrity and respect. To this end the development and responsible management of a Free Press, supported by Public Observance Panels, is seen as critical to the maintenance of a Democracy that is driven by Charitable endeavour.

Our purpose as a species is to investigate this thing called Life, constantly expanding our own potential in a never-ending cycle of trial and error that enables us to experience and learn. This can only function effectively within an environment of Integrity and Trust, something that is our collective responsibility to maintain and manage through a healthy Democratic process.

This collective responsibility is necessary in creating greater transparency in all we do, to protect the common good and avoid the continued abuse of each other and our Planet, something that is now threatening our very survival. This balance and credibility can be achieved by the development and responsible management of a Free Press, complemented by the principles that have driven our judicial jury service for centuries. Similarly-designed bodies (Public Observance Panels) would be able to bring an independent perspective that is charged with looking for signs of human fallibility in the organisations functioning within Society, whilst respecting the often sensitive nature of their activities. This is not spying (who are we spying for, other than ourselves?), but a healthy acknowledgement of human fallibility, as well as supporting the vested interests of Society. Broadening the traditional democratic process in this manner will testify to our recognition and acceptance of our purpose as a species, and the greater respect and esteem we achieve in better managing our fallibilities whilst pursuing our purpose.

6. There is a fundamental recognition of the vested interest of all people to be supported throughout the natural course of human life. This support comprises education and work, a home to rear a family and the enjoyment of the fruits of a supportive retirement, as well as being cared for in times of ill-health.

It is recognised that our time is the greatest gift we have to give in Life, because we can apportion it wherever we choose, unless placed under duress. The level of importance of the 'employment' of an employer or employee's time is the same; it is simply applied in different areas. No organisation could be built or function without the direction of the employer and the support of the employee, as both are integral to its structure. Better recognition of the rewards from the success of this joint employment of time can only move us beyond traditional practices that have often held Society to ransom. With a new belief that recognises the true gift of time, we bring new values into Society, elevating further the true worth of both employer and employee. It creates a vibrant social infrastructure through the natural circulation of our total commercial resources of time, money and materials. We recognise that everything is interdependent within this infrastructure, as a natural cycle of: Society and our Planet supporting Commerce and Commerce supporting Society and our Planet.

As a species, we are designed to constantly strive to achieve in every area of Life. As we grow old, the accumulation of our Life experiences from all of this striving represents a valuable store of wisdom. Here again, we see a natural cycle at work as we accept that, for the majority of our lives, we have been strong enough to support a family, an employer or employees, making a contribution to Society in the process. Now we look to that support being returned by a strong Society to its ageing contributors. We recognise and acknowledge the value of the contribution each person makes to this thing called 'Life' when we respect this natural cycle. We enter Life with nothing and leave it in the same fashion. This document champions the belief that the mark of a healthy Society is the extent to which we support each other and our Planet between these two events.

7. Our beliefs about Life, and our presence and purpose upon Planet Earth, come from a myriad of understandings that are identified by our Scientific, Spiritual and Religious institutions. As we merge into a fully-functioning Global community, it becomes necessary for us collectively to recognise and respect that this aspect of the human condition is integral to every inhabitant of this Planet. It is equally necessary to recognise respect and accept that, no matter which belief each one of us chooses, we have done so in the understanding that it brings the greatest succour and support in our constant confrontations with Life's challenges. Of all the Core Beliefs, this is intended as the most unifying.

For millennia, our religious and scientific beliefs have been the means to the attainment of power, through constant and bloody conflict that has cost the lives of countless millions of innocent people. As we integrate into a Global Village, we cannot help but better understand each other and increasingly recognise that it is the extremist views and actions of each belief system, be it political, commercial or religious, that are responsible for ongoing conflict and human suffering. If these belief systems are to retain the support of the people, they must recognise they are the means with which to persuade these extremist elements that their actions cannot achieve a meaningful outcome. The Internet is educating us all that peaceful protest is the bedrock from which lasting change occurs, and that violent conflict no longer frightens us but simply makes us more determined in our pursuit of a better Life.

8. This new mind-set recognises that our children are our future Society. Their full and rounded education, including the latest thinking in who and what we are and how we function as a species, is paramount to their positive interaction with each other as future Stewards of this Planet and the mechanism by which we, as a species, achieve World Peace.

Recognising that, as a species, we constantly test our boundaries throughout our lives, we provide an environment within which to shape the development of our young in their formative years. They face more challenges now than has ever been the case before in our history, due entirely to the multidimensional levels of complexity our current stage of Evolution is presenting us with. Providing an understanding on how we function in this thing called Life is essential to nurturing their ability to reach balanced judgements in how and where they will fit in to this new Global Society and the contribution they have to make. To this end, our traditional academic education should be expanded to encompass a fundamental understanding of our species and its relationship with Planet Earth. The final phase of their education would support their emergence into our infant multicultural Society. In this manner, they can enter Society fully understanding Society's boundaries and the healthy functioning of that Society. Of equal importance is the understanding that it is only in the education of our children that we can attain World Peace as a species, and that the resultant reductions in our military budgets would provide the ongoing means to finance future education programmes. We don't have a poverty of education or anything else, but a values problem in the priorities we apply to 'fighting' over 'living'.

9. Planet Earth is acknowledged as the sole supporter of human life. In recognising this, humanity seeks a new and sustainable relationship that reflects our dependence on the proper management of all Planetary resources. In so doing, we accept this Planet as our collective home and intimate benefactor of all we do ... Our Mate!

It was recognised and established that, by overcoming the general ignorance about whales through bringing people into closer contact with them, we were able to change attitudes, overcome apathy and reshape beliefs that sought to protect them. Only by adopting similar principles about our relationship to Planet Earth can we introduce a more supportive attitude to the positive management of its essential resources and benefit our future survival. A comprehensive review of our traditional belief systems about how our Planetary resources are utilised is therefore essential, as well as in the education of our young. Included within this reappraisal is the understanding that food and water resources are ring-fenced from commercial priorities. This would include the gradual phasing out of beliefs that do not encourage the nurture of this Planet and its healthy maintenance.

10. This document is dedicated to the greater empowerment of our species and furthering a more caring Society, both locally and globally. To this end, there is a commitment, within Society, to elevate and prioritise the support of the many organisations, charities and independent bodies that are already pioneering this task across the broad spectrum of human activity.

The belief systems operated by these organisations worldwide is the key ingredient to the ways and means by which our species might tackle the looming food and water crisis. Global Magna Carta is therefore humbly offered as the vehicle to support their greater involvement in the political and democratic process, as a means of enhancing the attainment of their individual core objectives and the vast contribution this will make to our future survival.

A Tribute to Humanity

Global Magna Carta pays tribute to Humanity and what an incredible species we are. Only by collectively recognising our need to take control of our Evolutionary process, and manage the changes inherent within that process, can we minimise tragic human conflict that is wasted in our futile attempts to resist this constant change.

It is never what happens that is important

But how we deal with it ... Always.

JTC, OCTOBER 2013

The Magna Carta (The Great Charter)

Abuses by King John caused a revolt by nobles, who compelled him to execute this recognition of rights for both noblemen and ordinary Englishmen. It established the principle that no one, including the king or a lawmaker, is above the law.

Preamble: John, by the grace of God, king of England, lord of Ireland, duke of Normandy and Aquitaine, and count of Anjou, to the archbishop, bishops, abbots, earls, barons, justiciaries, foresters, sheriffs, stewards, servants, and to all his bailiffs and liege subjects, greetings. Know that, having regard to God and for the salvation of our soul, and those of all our ancestors and heirs, and unto the honor of God and the advancement of his holy Church and for the rectifying of our realm, we have granted as underwritten by advice of our venerable fathers, Stephen, archbishop of Canterbury, primate of all England and cardinal of the holy Roman Church, Henry, archbishop of Dublin, William of London, Peter of Winchester, Jocelyn of Bath and Glastonbury, Hugh of Lincoln, Walter of Worcester, William of Coventry, Benedict of Rochester, bishops of Master Pandulf, subdeacon and member of the household of our lord the Pope, of brother Aymeric (master of the Knights of the Temple in England), and of the illustrious men William Marshal, earl of Pembroke, William, earl of Salisbury, William, earl of Warenne, William, earl of Arundel, Alan of Galloway (constable of Scotland), Waren Fitz Gerold, Peter Fitz Herbert, Hubert De Burgh (seneschal of Poitou), Hugh de Neville, Matthew Fitz Herbert, Thomas Basset, Alan Basset, Philip d'Aubigny, Robert of Roppesley, John Marshal, John Fitz Hugh, and others, our liegemen.

1. In the first place we have granted to God, and by this our present charter confirmed for us and our heirs forever that the English Church shall be free, and shall have her rights entire, and her liberties inviolate; and we will that it be thus observed; which is apparent from this that the freedom of elections, which is reckoned most important and very essential to the English Church, we, of our pure and unconstrained will, did grant, and did by our charter confirm and did obtain the ratification of the same from our lord, Pope Innocent III, before the quarrel arose between us and our barons: and this we will observe, and our will is that it be observed in good faith by our heirs forever. We have also granted to all freemen of our kingdom, for us and our heirs forever, all the underwritten liberties, to be had and held by them and their heirs, of us and our heirs forever.

2. If any of our earls or barons, or others holding of us in chief by military service shall have died, and at the time of his death his heir shall be full of age and owe 'relief', he shall have his inheritance by the old relief, to wit, the heir or heirs of

an earl, for the whole barony of an earl by £100; the heir or heirs of a baron, £100 for a whole barony; the heir or heirs of a knight, 100s, at most, and whoever owes less let him give less, according to the ancient custom of fees.

3. If, however, the heir of any one of the aforesaid has been under age and in wardship, let him have his inheritance without relief and without fine when he comes of age.
4. The guardian of the land of an heir who is thus under age, shall take from the land of the heir nothing but reasonable produce, reasonable customs, and reasonable services, and that without destruction or waste of men or goods; and if we have committed the wardship of the lands of any such minor to the sheriff, or to any other who is responsible to us for its issues, and he has made destruction or waster of what he holds in wardship, we will take of him amends, and the land shall be committed to two lawful and discreet men of that fee, who shall be responsible for the issues to us or to him to whom we shall assign them; and if we have given or sold the wardship of any such land to anyone and he has therein made destruction or waste, he shall lose that wardship, and it shall be transferred to two lawful and discreet men of that fief, who shall be responsible to us in like manner as aforesaid.
5. The guardian, moreover, so long as he has the wardship of the land, shall keep up the houses, parks, fishponds, stanks, mills, and other things pertaining to the land, out of the issues of the same land; and he shall restore to the heir, when he has come to full age, all his land, stocked with ploughs and wainage, according as the season of husbandry shall require, and the issues of the land can reasonable bear.
6. Heirs shall be married without disparagement, yet so that before the marriage takes place the nearest in blood to that heir shall have notice.
7. A widow, after the death of her husband, shall forthwith and without difficulty have her marriage portion and inheritance; nor shall she give anything for her dower, or for her marriage portion, or for the inheritance which her husband and she held on the day of the death of that husband; and she may remain in the house of her husband for forty days after his death, within which time her dower shall be assigned to her.
8. No widow shall be compelled to marry, so long as she prefers to live without a husband; provided always that she gives security not to marry without our consent, if she holds of us, or without the consent of the lord of whom she holds, if she holds of another.

9. Neither we nor our bailiffs will seize any land or rent for any debt, as long as the chattels of the debtor are sufficient to repay the debt; nor shall the sureties of the debtor be distrained so long as the principal debtor is able to satisfy the debt; and if the principal debtor shall fail to pay the debt, having nothing wherewith to pay it, then the sureties shall answer for the debt; and let them have the lands and rents of the debtor, if they desire them, until they are indemnified for the debt which they have paid for him, unless the principal debtor can show proof that he is discharged thereof as against the said sureties.
10. If one who has borrowed from the Jews any sum, great or small, die before that loan be repaid, the debt shall not bear interest while the heir is under age, of whomsoever he may hold; and if the debt fall into our hands, we will not take anything except the principal sum contained in the bond.
11. And if anyone die indebted to the Jews, his wife shall have her dower and pay nothing of that debt; and if any children of the deceased are left under age, necessaries shall be provided for them in keeping with the holding of the deceased; and out of the residue the debt shall be paid, reserving, however, service due to feudal lords; in like manner let it be done touching debts due to others than Jews.
12. No scutage not aid shall be imposed on our kingdom, unless by common counsel of our kingdom, except for ransoming our person, for making our eldest son a knight, and for once marrying our eldest daughter; and for these there shall not be levied more than a reasonable aid. In like manner it shall be done concerning aids from the city of London.
13. And the city of London shall have all it ancient liberties and free customs, as well by land as by water; furthermore, we decree and grant that all other cities, boroughs, towns, and ports shall have all their liberties and free customs.
14. And for obtaining the common counsel of the kingdom anent the assessing of an aid (except in the three cases aforesaid) or of a scutage, we will cause to be summoned the archbishops, bishops, abbots, earls, and greater barons, severally by our letters; and we will moreover cause to be summoned generally, through our sheriffs and bailiffs, and others who hold of us in chief, for a fixed date, namely, after the expiry of at least forty days, and at a fixed place; and in all letters of such summons we will specify the reason of the summons. And when the summons has thus been made, the business shall proceed on the day appointed, according to the counsel of such as are present, although not all who were summoned have come.

15. We will not for the future grant to anyone license to take an aid from his own free tenants, except to ransom his person, to make his eldest son a knight, and once to marry his eldest daughter; and on each of these occasions there shall be levied only a reasonable aid.
16. No one shall be distrained for performance of greater service for a knight's fee, or for any other free tenement, than is due therefrom.
17. Common pleas shall not follow our court, but shall be held in some fixed place.
18. Inquests of novel disseisin, of mort d'ancestor, and of darrein presentment shall not be held elsewhere than in their own county courts, and that in manner following. We, or, if we should be out of the realm, our chief justiciar, will send two justiciaries through every county four times a year, who shall alone with four knights of the county chosen by the county, hold the said assizes in the county court, on the day and in the place of meeting of that court.
19. And if any of the said assizes cannot be taken on the day of the county court, let there remain of the knights and freeholders, who were present at the county court on that day, as many as may be required for the efficient making of judgments, according as the business be more or less.
20. A freeman shall not be amerced for a slight offense, except in accordance with the degree of the offense; and for a grave offense he shall be amerced in accordance with the gravity of the offense, yet saving always his 'contentment'; and a merchant in the same way, saving his 'merchandise'; and a villein shall be amerced in the same way, saving his 'wainage' if they have fallen into our mercy: and none of the aforesaid amercements shall be imposed except by the oath of honest men of the neighbourhood.
21. Earls and barons shall not be amerced except through their peers, and only in accordance with the degree of the offense.
22. A clerk shall not be amerced in respect of his lay holding except after the manner of the others aforesaid; further, he shall not be amerced in accordance with the extent of his ecclesiastical benefice.
23. No village or individual shall be compelled to make bridges at river banks, except those who from of old were legally bound to do so.
24. No sheriff, constable, coroners, or others of our bailiffs, shall hold pleas of our Crown.
25. All counties, hundred, wapentakes, and trithings (except our demesne manors) shall remain at the old rents, and without any additional payment.

26. If anyone holding of us a lay fief shall die, and our sheriff or bailiff shall exhibit our letters patent of summons for a debt which the deceased owed us, it shall be lawful for our sheriff or bailiff to attach and enrol the chattels of the deceased, found upon the lay fief, to the value of that debt, at the sight of law worthy men, provided always that nothing whatever be thence removed until the debt which is evident shall be fully paid to us; and the residue shall be left to the executors to fulfil the will of the deceased; and if there be nothing due from him to us, all the chattels shall go to the deceased, saving to his wife and children their reasonable shares.

27. If any freeman shall die intestate, his chattels shall be distributed by the hands of his nearest kinsfolk and friends, under supervision of the Church, saving to every one the debts which the deceased owed to him.

28. No constable or other bailiff of ours shall take corn or other provisions from anyone without immediately tendering money therefor, unless he can have postponement thereof by permission of the seller.

29. No constable shall compel any knight to give money in lieu of castle-guard, when he is willing to perform it in his own person, or (if he himself cannot do it from any reasonable cause) then by another responsible man. Further, if we have led or sent him upon military service, he shall be relieved from guard in proportion to the time during which he has been on service because of us.

30. No sheriff or bailiff of ours, or other person, shall take the horses or carts of any freeman for transport duty, against the will of the said freeman.

31. Neither we nor our bailiffs shall take, for our castles or for any other work of ours, wood which is not ours, against the will of the owner of that wood.

32. We will not retain beyond one year and one day, the lands those who have been convicted of felony, and the lands shall thereafter be handed over to the lords of the fiefs.

33. All kydells for the future shall be removed altogether from Thames and Medway, and throughout all England, except upon the seashore.

34. The writ which is called praecipe shall not for the future be issued to anyone, regarding any tenement whereby a freeman may lose his court.

35. Let there be one measure of wine throughout our whole realm; and one measure of ale; and one measure of corn, to wit, 'the London quarter'; and one width of cloth (whether dyed, or russet, or 'halberget'), to wit, two ells within the selvedges; of weights also let it be as of measures.

36. Nothing in future shall be given or taken for a writ of inquisition of life or limbs, but freely it shall be granted, and never denied.

37. If anyone holds of us by fee-farm, either by socage or by burage, or of any other land by knight's service, we will not (by reason of that fee-farm, socage, or burgage), have the wardship of the heir, or of such land of his as if of the fief of that other; nor shall we have wardship of that fee-farm, socage, or burgage, unless such fee-farm owes knight's service. We will not by reason of any small serjeancy which anyone may hold of us by the service of rendering to us knives, arrows, or the like, have wardship of his heir or of the land which he holds of another lord by knight's service.

38. No bailiff for the future shall, upon his own unsupported complaint, put anyone to his 'law', without credible witnesses brought for this purposes.

39. No freemen shall be taken or imprisoned or disseised or exiled or in any way destroyed, nor will we go upon him nor send upon him, except by the lawful judgment of his peers or by the law of the land.

40. To no one will we sell, to no one will we refuse or delay, right or justice.

41. All merchants shall have safe and secure exit from England, and entry to England, with the right to tarry there and to move about as well by land as by water, for buying and selling by the ancient and right customs, quit from all evil tolls, except (in time of war) such merchants as are of the land at war with us. And if such are found in our land at the beginning of the war, they shall be detained, without injury to their bodies or goods, until information be received by us, or by our chief justiciar, how the merchants of our land found in the land at war with us are treated; and if our men are safe there, the others shall be safe in our land.

42. It shall be lawful in future for anyone (excepting always those imprisoned or outlawed in accordance with the law of the kingdom, and natives of any country at war with us, and merchants, who shall be treated as if above provided) to leave our kingdom and to return, safe and secure by land and water, except for a short period in time of war, on grounds of public policy – reserving always the allegiance due to us.

43. If anyone holding of some escheat (such as the honour of Wallingford, Nottingham, Boulogne, Lancaster, or of other escheats which are in our hands and are baronies) shall die, his heir shall give no other relief, and perform no other service to us than he would have done to the baron if that barony had been in the baron's hand; and we shall hold it in the same manner in which the baron held it.

44. Men who dwell without the forest need not henceforth come before our justiciaries of the forest upon a general summons, unless they are in plea, or sureties of one or more, who are attached for the forest.
45. We will appoint as justices, constables, sheriffs, or bailiffs only such as know the law of the realm and mean to observe it well.
46. All barons who have founded abbeys, concerning which they hold charters from the kings of England, or of which they have long continued possession, shall have the wardship of them, when vacant, as they ought to have.
47. All forests that have been made such in our time shall forthwith be disafforsted; and a similar course shall be followed with regard to river banks that have been placed 'in defense' by us in our time.
48. All evil customs connected with forests and warrens, foresters and warreners, sheriffs and their officers, river banks and their wardens, shall immediately by inquired into in each county by twelve sworn knights of the same county chosen by the honest men of the same county, and shall, within forty days of the said inquest, be utterly abolished, so as never to be restored, provided always that we previously have intimation thereof, or our justiciar, if we should not be in England.
49. We will immediately restore all hostages and charters delivered to us by Englishmen, as sureties of the peace of faithful service.
50. We will entirely remove from their bailiwicks, the relations of Gerard of Athee (so that in future they shall have no bailiwick in England); namely, Engelard of Cigogne, Peter, Guy, and Andrew of Chanceaux, Guy of Cigogne, Geoffrey of Martigny with his brothers, Philip Mark with his brothers and his nephew Geoffrey, and the whole brood of the same.
51. As soon as peace is restored, we will banish from the kingdom all foreign born knights, crossbowmen, serjeants, and mercenary soldiers who have come with horses and arms to the kingdom's hurt.
52. If anyone has been dispossessed or removed by us, without the legal judgment of his peers, from his lands, castles, franchises, or from his right, we will immediately restore them to him; and if a dispute arise over this, then let it be decided by the five and twenty barons of whom mention is made below in the clause for securing the peace. Moreover, for all those possessions, from which anyone has, without the lawful judgment of his peers, been disseised or removed, by our father, King Henry, or by our brother, King Richard, and

which we retain in our hand (or which as possessed by others, to whom we are bound to warrant them) we shall have respite until the usual term of crusaders; excepting those things about which a plea has been raised, or an inquest made by our order, before our taking of the cross; but as soon as we return from the expedition, we will immediately grant full justice therein.

53. We shall have, moreover, the same respite and in the same manner in rendering justice concerning the disafforestation or retention of those forests which Henry our father and Richard our brother afforested, and concerning the wardship of lands which are of the fief of another (namely, such wardships as we have hitherto had by reason of a fief which anyone held of us by knight's service), and concerning abbeys founded on other fiefs than our own, in which the lord of the fee claims to have right; and when we have returned, or if we desist from our expedition, we will immediately grant full justice to all who complain of such things.

54. No one shall be arrested or imprisoned upon the appeal of a woman, for the death of any other than her husband.

55. All fines made with us unjustly and against the law of the land, and all amercements, imposed unjustly and against the law of the land, shall be entirely remitted, or else it shall be done concerning them according to the decision of the five and twenty barons whom mention is made below in the clause for securing the pease, or according to the judgment of the majority of the same, along with the aforesaid Stephen, archbishop of Canterbury, if he can be present, and such others as he may wish to bring with him for this purpose, and if he cannot be present the business shall nevertheless proceed without him, provided always that if any one or more of the aforesaid five and twenty barons are in a similar suit, they shall be removed as far as concerns this particular judgment, others being substituted in their places after having been selected by the rest of the same five and twenty for this purpose only, and after having been sworn.

56. If we have disseised or removed Welshmen from lands or liberties, or other things, without the legal judgment of their peers in England or in Wales, they shall be immediately restored to them; and if a dispute arise over this, then let it be decided in the marches by the judgment of their peers; for the tenements in England according to the law of England, for tenements in Wales according to the law of Wales, and for tenements in the marches according to the law of the marches. Welshmen shall do the same to us and ours.

57. Further, for all those possessions from which any Welshman has, without the lawful judgment of his peers, been disseised or removed by King Henry our father, or King Richard our brother, and which we retain in our hand (or which are possessed by others, and which we ought to warrant), we will have respite until the usual term of crusaders; excepting those things about which a plea has been raised or an inquest made by our order before we took the cross; but as soon as we return (or if perchance we desist from our expedition), we will immediately grant full justice in accordance with the laws of the Welsh and in relation to the foresaid regions.
58. We will immediately give up the son of Llywelyn and all the hostages of Wales, and the charters delivered to us as security for the peace.
59. We will do towards Alexander, king of Scots, concerning the return of his sisters and his hostages, and concerning his franchises, and his right, in the same manner as we shall do towards our other barons of England, unless it ought to be otherwise according to the charters which we hold from William his father, formerly king of Scots; and this shall be according to the judgment of his peers in our court.
60. Moreover, all these aforesaid customs and liberties, the observances of which we have granted in our kingdom as far as pertains to us towards our men, shall be observed by all of our kingdom, as well clergy as laymen, as far as pertains to them towards their men.
61. Since, moreover, for God and the amendment of our kingdom and for the better allaying of the quarrel that has arisen between us and our barons, we have granted all these concessions, desirous that they should enjoy them in complete and firm endurance forever, we give and grant to them the underwritten security, namely, that the barons choose five and twenty barons of the kingdom, whomsoever they will, who shall be bound with all their might, to observe and hold, and cause to be observed, the peace and liberties we have granted and confirmed to them by this our present Charter, so that if we, or our justiciar, or our bailiffs or any one of our officers, shall in anything be at fault towards anyone, or shall have broken any one of the articles of this peace or of this security, and the offense be notified to four barons of the foresaid five and twenty, the said four barons shall repair to us (or our justiciar, if we are out of the realm) and, laying the transgression before us, petition to have that transgression redressed without delay. And if we shall not have corrected the transgression (or, in the event of our being out of the realm, if our justiciar shall not have corrected it) within forty days, reckoning from the time it has been

intimated to us (or to our justiciar, if we should be out of the realm), the four barons aforesaid shall refer that matter to the rest of the five and twenty barons, and those five and twenty barons shall, together with the community of the whole realm, distrain and distress us in all possible ways, namely, by seizing our castles, lands, possessions, and in any other way they can, until redress has been obtained as they deem fit, saving harmless our own person, and the persons of our queen and children; and when redress has been obtained, they shall resume their old relations towards us. And let whoever in the country desires it, swear to obey the orders of the said five and twenty barons for the execution of all the aforesaid matters, and along with them, to molest us to the utmost of his power; and we publicly and freely grant leave to everyone who wishes to swear, and we shall never forbid anyone to swear. All those, moreover, in the land who of themselves and of their own accord are unwilling to swear to the twenty five to help them in constraining and molesting us, we shall by our command compel the same to swear to the effect foresaid. And if any one of the five and twenty barons shall have died or departed from the land, or be incapacitated in any other manner which would prevent the foresaid provisions being carried out, those of the said twenty five barons who are left shall choose another in his place according to their own judgment, and he shall be sworn in the same way as the others. Further, in all matters, the execution of which is entrusted, to these twenty five barons, if perchance these twenty five are present and disagree about anything, or if some of them, after being summoned, are unwilling or unable to be present, that which the majority of those present ordain or command shall be held as fixed and established, exactly as if the whole twenty five had concurred in this; and the said twenty five shall swear that they will faithfully observe all that is aforesaid, and cause it to be observed with all their might. And we shall procure nothing from anyone, directly or indirectly, whereby any part of these concessions and liberties might be revoked or diminished; and if any such things has been procured, let it be void and null, and we shall never use it personally or by another.

62. And all the will, hatreds, and bitterness that have arisen between us and our men, clergy and lay, from the date of the quarrel, we have completely remitted and pardoned to everyone. Moreover, all trespasses occasioned by the said quarrel, from Easter in the sixteenth year of our reign till the restoration of peace, we have fully remitted to all, both clergy and laymen, and completely forgiven, as far as pertains to us. And on this head, we have caused to be made for them letters testimonial patent of the lord Stephen, archbishop of Canterbury, of the lord Henry, archbishop of Dublin, of the bishops aforesaid, and of Master Pandulf as touching this security and the concessions aforesaid.

63. Wherefore we will and firmly order that the English Church be free, and that the men in our kingdom have and hold all the aforesaid liberties, rights, and concessions, well and peaceably, freely and quietly, fully and wholly, for themselves and their heirs, of us and our heirs, in all respects and in all places forever, as is aforesaid. An oath, moreover, has been taken, as well on our part as on the art of the barons, that all these conditions aforesaid shall be kept in good faith and without evil intent.

Given under our hand – the above named and many others being witnesses – in the meadow which is called Runnymede, between Windsor and Staines, on the fifteenth day of June, in the seventeenth year of our reign.

Prepared by Nancy Troutman (The Cleveland Free-Net – aa345). Distributed by the Cybercasting Services Division of the National Public Telecomputing Network (NPTN). http://www.constitution.org/eng/magnacar.htm

> *This is but one of three different translations I found of the Magna Carta; it was originally written in Latin, probably by the Archbishop, Stephen Langton. It was in force for only a few months, when it was violated by the king. Just over a year later, with no resolution to the war, the king died, being succeeded by his 9-year old son, Henry III. The Charter (Carta) was reissued again, with some revisions, in 1216, 1217 and 1225. As near as I can tell, the version presented here is the one that preceded all of the others; nearly all of its provisions were soon superseded by other laws, and none of it is effective today. The two other versions I found each professed to be the original, as well. The basic intent of each is the same.*
>
> GERALD MURPHY, THE CLEVELAND FREE-NET – AA300

A JOKE TO FINISH WITH

Life is far too important a thing ever to talk seriously about.

OSCAR WILDE

When Marlon Brando made the film Last Tango in Paris, it was reported that on the set of the first erotic scene there was extreme tension at the prospect of what had to be portrayed. When he entered the set, to join his beautiful co-star, Maria Schneider, the star was wearing the minimum of clothing along with *wellington boots,* which he kept on throughout that and subsequent similar scenes. (I have *adjusted* some of the detail about this "wellington boot story" to help make a powerful point.)

... And that point?

It is our bounden duty, like Marlon Brando, to realise as much of our limitless potential as we can through recognising our strengths and weaknesses. This includes our duty to remain *grounded* in the humility of knowing who and what we are, as well as exercising great respect for this beautiful Planet and all of its wonderful Inhabitants.

I believe that Life is a huge playground in which we can do whatever we like, as we go about the task of experiencing the limitless ways we can apply our talents to living Life.

The only ground rules are those which take the shape of *Universal Disciplines,* as I call them. They do not seek to inhibit our ability to create, that is fundamental to us, but they do impose disciplines that provide an insight into what we are doing, rather than stopping us from doing them.

They cannot be manipulated by us or bent to conform to our impulses and fallibilities; in this respect, they can be utterly ruthless, when it is necessary for us to learn a bit more about us and our playground. *Our collective Wellington Boots!*

We have just experienced our disrespect for *Integrity* and this may teach us the futility of fighting against it. There are other Universal Disciplines that also operate. The trick, as with anything in Life, is to work with them rather than against them.

I began my observations with a joke, which highlighted the circumstances surrounding much of what I have to say. In spite of the seriousness of the subject matter, I believe it is also right to finish with a joke (of which the story may or may not be true), that highlights our need to never lose the ability to laugh at ourselves.

We are imbued with a sense of humour as a *leveller* to our excesses, offering a powerful mirror with which to recognise, respect and better manage our fallibilities. Our current obsession with financialising Life has deadened this critically important tool, thwarting our ability to remain humble and in awe of the wonder that is Life on Planet Earth.

The *uniforms* of the nations in this joke are unimportant; they could be any two nations on this Planet. It is the interactions that create the humour that points to our fallibilities.

Here, we see human ego at work as it drives relentlessly to its own potential destruction, resisting immoveable forces it is not prepared to recognise.

It is this last point that highlights the value of humour as the most perceptive form of constructive criticism. It stimulates a deep-seated need within all of us to recognise and acknowledge the futility of transgressing the Natural order that is the Evolutionary process, constantly at work in Life.

What follows is the transcript of a radio conversation between the authorities of two countries during a naval training exercise somewhere in the world. The countries have previously been portrayed as US/British/Irish/Canadian ... and perhaps even more. However, it is really irrelevant for the purpose of this story! Enjoy.

1st Country: Please divert your course 15 degrees to the South to avoid a collision.

2nd Country: Recommend you divert your course 15 degrees to the North.

1st Country: Negative. You will have to divert your course 15 degrees to the South to avoid a collision.

2nd Country: This is the Captain of xxxxxxx Navy ship. I say again, divert YOUR course.

1st Country: No. I say again, you divert YOUR course.

2nd Country: THIS IS THE AIRCRAFT CARRIER XXXXXXXXX. THE SECOND LARGEST SHIP IN THE ATLANTIC FLEET. WE ARE ACCOMPANIED BY THREE DESTROYERS, THREE CRUISERS, AND NUMEROUS SUPPORT VESSELS.

I DEMAND THAT YOU CHANGE YOUR COURSE 15 DEGREES NORTH, I SAY AGAIN, THAT'S ONE FIVE DEGREES NORTH, OR COUNTERMEASURES WILL BE UNDERTAKEN TO ENSURE THE SAFETY OF THIS SHIP.

1st Country: We are a lighthouse ... Your call.

AUTHOR'S POSTSCRIPT

And so, dear reader, having got this far it is incumbent upon me to offer my sincere gratitude for the most precious of gifts we have to give during the course of our lives here on Earth, and something you have generously bestowed upon me in reading this book ... your time.

I am sure there are those who would question my right and validity to comment on such a broad spectrum of current human activity. Indeed, there are those who will seek to undermine this work by either attacking my character (I have certainly given them enough ammunition at the beginning!) or the validity of what I have to say. The former achieves nothing and the latter, done constructively, could offer valuable contributions to public debate. I have neither degrees in any of the *ologies,* nor a Doctorate in human behavioural sciences, and yet I believe my right and validity to speak is unquestionable ... *I live here and I care.*

www.ingramcontent.com/pod-product-compliance
Ingram Content Group UK Ltd.
Pitfield, Milton Keynes, MK11 3LW, UK
UKHW020133250726
13967UKWH00002B/625

9 780992 778217